S0-AXT-595

The Soviet Union and
the Gulf in the 1980s

SEN
187

The Soviet Union and
the Gulf in the 1980s

Carol R. Saivetz

Westview Press
BOULDER, SAN FRANCISCO, & LONDON

DS
326
S34
1989

ROBERT MANNING
STROZIER LIBRARY

SEP 14 1989

Tallahassee, Florida

Westview Special Studies in International Relations

This Westview softcover edition is printed on acid-free paper and bound in softcovers that carry the highest rating of the National Association of State Textbook Administrators, in consultation with the Association of American Publishers and the Book Manufacturers' Institute.

All rights reserved. No part of this publication may be reproduced or transmitted in any form or by any means, electronic or mechanical, including photocopy, recording, or any information storage and retrieval system, without permission in writing from the publisher.

Copyright © 1989 by Westview Press, Inc.

Published in 1989 in the United States of America by Westview Press, Inc., 5500 Central Avenue, Boulder, Colorado 80301, and in the United Kingdom by Westview Press, Inc., 13 Brunswick Centre, London WC1N 1AF, England

Library of Congress Cataloging-in-Publication Data
Saivetz, Carol R.
  The Soviet Union and the Gulf in the 1980s/Carol R. Saivetz.
    p. cm.—(Westview special studies in international
relations)
  Bibliography: p.
  Includes index.
  ISBN 0-8133-7072-8
  1. Persian Gulf Region—Foreign relations—Soviet Union.
2. Soviet Union—Foreign relations—Persian Gulf Region. 3. Iraqi-
Iranian Conflict. 1980–   . I. Title. II. Series.
DS326.S34 1989
327.47053'6—dc19   88-27000
                                                                        CIP

Printed and bound in the United States of America

The paper used in this publication meets the requirements of the American National Standard for Permanence of Paper for Printed Library Materials Z39.48-1984.

10   9   8   7   6   5   4   3   2   1

For My Parents

Contents

5 Conclusion: The Soviets and the Gulf   99

Illustrations

Acknowledgments

I would like to thank Robert O. Freedman and Lyn Ekedahl for their comments and suggestions on earlier drafts of the manuscript. I would also like to acknowledge the research assistance of David Kramer, Astrid Tuminez, and Allison Yenkin. Elizabeth Taylor provided valuable technical help. Most of all, my family provided moral support and are to be thanked for their patience.

Carol R. Saivetz

Base 503683 3-78

Introduction

Soviet interest in the Gulf is not a product of the crises of the seventies and eighties—the Iranian revolution, the invasion of Afghanistan, and the Iran–Iraq War—alone. Rather, the area has long been of vital interest to Moscow. In the 1800s, Russia's southward expansion brought the Tsarist empire not only to the Iranian border, but also to the point of direct involvement in Persian domestic affairs. By the turn of the century, Iran became a pawn in the Anglo–Russian chess game then being played out in Asia. The two rivals for regional power signed a convention in 1907 that divided the country into British and Tsarist spheres of influence and in 1908, Russian troops crossed the border.

The partition agreement remained in force until the Bolshevik revolution. Then, the new government under Vladimir I. Lenin renounced all Tsarist treaties and announced a new basis for its foreign policy dealings. After a short-lived attempt to establish the Soviet Republic of Gilan in northern Iran, Lenin opted instead for a treaty with the central government in Teheran. The treaty, one of the first three with what are now called Third World countries, included mutual pledges not to join military alliances against the other and not to permit hostile forces to operate from the other's territory. And in a clause originally directed against Tsarist forces then still operating in Iran, Russia reserved the right to intervene in Iran "for the purposes of carrying out the necessary military operations in the interests of its defenses."[1]

In the late twenties, Stalin's Russia was preoccupied with European politics and, in the thirties, with the growing German military strength. When attempts at collective security failed, Stalin ultimately entered into a nonaggression pact with Nazi Germany. During the period of the Nazi–Soviet Nonaggression Pact (1939–1941), the Soviets reportedly indicated their interest in territories to their south, including Iran and Turkey. But it was the Nazi attack on the USSR in June 1941 that provided Moscow with an opportunity to place its troops in Iran. During the war, the pro-German leanings of Reza Shah prompted almost a repeat performance of 1907 from both the USSR and Great Britain. They agreed to occupy Iran jointly for the duration of the war. At the time, Reza Shah abdicated in favor of his son and the young

Shah forced the USSR and Britain to sign a formal occupation agreement. In 1945, the British withdrew as stipulated in the agreement, while the Soviets remained entrenched in northern Iran. Additionally, the Tudeh (communist) Party proclaimed the independence of Azerbaijan—an area adjacent to the USSR. In what became one of the first Cold War crises, the United Nations Security Council urged both Teheran and Moscow to negotiate. Ultimately, Iran "bought out" the Soviets by agreeing to establish a joint Soviet-Iranian oil company (subject to the approval of the Majlis) in return for Soviet withdrawal. When the Soviets withdrew, Teheran crushed the rebellion in Azerbaijan, and in the end, the Majlis refused to grant Moscow the promised concessions.

This early East–West confrontation in the Gulf notwithstanding, it was not until Stalin's death in March 1953 that the Soviet Union directed its attention to the Third World. Under Khrushchev, Soviet links to the Third World proliferated. In the Gulf region, the USSR established ties to the military rulers of Iraq, the Imam of Yemen, and sought to constrain—if possible—the Shah of Iran's relations with the United States. The Kremlin's involvement in regional affairs expanded again in the sixties. Moscow provided military and logistical assistance to the republican forces during the Yemen civil war, supported the new Marxist government in Aden, and established firm economic and even military ties with the Shah. By the seventies, the USSR had signed a Friendship and Cooperation Treaty with Iraq and a 15-year economic agreement with Iran. In other parts of the Arabian Peninsula, ties were strengthened with Aden, the Yemen Arab Republic, and Kuwait. None of these bilateral ties was without its tensions; but, the Soviets were satisfied with the extent of their presence in the region.

It is against this background that current Soviet interest and involvement in the region must be understood. The USSR is clearly concerned with its security and the propinquity of the Gulf dictates that Moscow watch events there carefully. As spokesman after spokesman has stated: The USSR must be concerned about a region so close to its borders. In addition, over the years of Soviet involvement in the Third World, Moscow has definitely been aware of the geostrategic value of particular territories. The assumption that the Soviets recognize the political and strategic importance of the Gulf also carries with it .the negative corollary of attempting to deny these advantages to the West. Thus Soviet policy has been designed to counter Western influence positions and to court native anti-Americanism.

The strategic value of the Gulf and the Soviet desire to lessen Western influence there cannot be considered without mention of oil. The rich oil reserves of Iran, Iraq, and the Arabian Peninsula certainly enhanced the region's strategic and political value. Indeed, over the past several years, instability in the Gulf, Soviet proximity to the area, and speculation about Soviet oil reserves have evoked alarm in the West about possible Kremlin control of Middle East oil. In 1977, the CIA estimated that the USSR would become a net importer of oil by the mid-1980s. Did this mean that Moscow would drive toward the Gulf to ensure its own supply? It is of course plausible to consider that Moscow might also move to establish a stable, long-term economic relationship with a major oil exporter in order to secure supply. While this remains a policy option, more recent studies criticized the CIA estimates and argued that the Soviets would continue to have an adequate oil supply for years to come.

That the Soviets do not necessarily need oil does not preclude arguments regarding Soviet desires to control the spigot. Other Western analysts contend that Soviet interest in the Gulf is dictated in large measure by the wish to choke off the West's supply of oil. While both reasons certainly enhance Soviet interest in the region, control of the area's oil or at least access to it would seem to be a by-product and not the prime motivation for Soviet involvement. In fact, Moscow's efforts to become a regional power through oil—that is its approaches to the oil producers for meetings and coordination of prices—have largely been rebuffed. By the same token, the Soviets recently have shown themselves to be responsive to requests from Iran to regulate output.

Finally, Moscow has also approached Third World politics with a marked desire for superpower status. Following former foreign minister Andrei Gromyko's oft-cited dictum that no question can be decided without Soviet input, the Kremlin has indicated its resolve to participate in regional politics across the globe. In the Gulf, Moscow has called for an end to the Iran-Iraq War, attempted its own mediation efforts, and supplied arms directly and indirectly to the combatants.

For all these reasons, the Gulf is an area of major concern to Kremlin policy-makers. Beginning in the late seventies, events in the region and its periphery were to create significant policy dilemmas. In February 1979, Iran underwent a revolution that was to have a profound impact on the Middle East and on the superpowers. For the Soviets, the Islamic revolution in Iran posed problems on both the theoretical/ ideological and practical levels. Not only did Moscow have to explain the role of the clergy and Shi'ism, but it also had to contend with both the potential disruption in the fabric of Soviet–Iranian relations and the Khomeini policy of exporting Islamic fundamentalism. The USSR had less than a year to adjust to the new set of Iranian circumstances when events in the region presented new dilemmas for policy makers.

The Kremlin leadership confronted first the deteriorating situation in Afghanistan which led to the 1979 Christmas time Soviet invasion. Then, the historic rivalry between neighbors Iran and Iraq exploded into open warfare.

The Afghan invasion and continuing Soviet occupation constitute a large component of the backdrop to Soviet policy toward the Gulf War. A discussion of Afghani politics and of the history of Soviet involvement in Kabul is beyond the scope of this study.[2] In short, the communist coup of April 1978 brought to power a badly divided leadership which pursued policies that were detrimental to its ability to consolidate its hold on power. Internal armed resistance to the government intensified, presenting Moscow with a policy problem: Could the Kremlin afford to allow a communist government on its borders to fall to insurgents without damaging its image as "supersocialist?" The Soviets apparently concluded that decisive action was necessary: Soviet troops crossed into Afghanistan on December 24, 1979, and for the next two days, transport planes ferried soldiers to the Afghan capital.

Washington policy makers, confronted with the collapse of the Shah and Khomeini's virulent anti-Americanism, viewed the Soviet occupation of Afghanistan as a major Soviet thrust into the Gulf. If nothing else, Soviet troops were now several hundreds of kilometers closer than before to the oil supply of the Arabian Peninsula. President Jimmy Carter, making note of the changed regional balance, said in his 1980 State of the Union Address: "An attempt by any outside force to gain control of the Persian Gulf region will be regarded as an assault on the vital interest of the United States of America, and such an assault will be repelled by any means necessary, including military force."[3] He directed the Joint Chiefs of Staff to develop a mobile, easily and quickly deployable force which could be used to counter the Soviet threat. President Carter also initiated a move to boycott the 1980 olympic games scheduled for Moscow.

Against the backdrop of the Islamic revolution and the Soviet occupation of Afghanistan, the outbreak of the Iran–Iraq War provided new opportunities and new dilemmas for Moscow. In other instances, regional conflicts had provided avenues of entree to the Soviets: By proffering arms and/or verbal, diplomatic support to one of two combatants, the Kremlin successfully cultivated new clients or proved continuing support to old friends. Despite the good relations between Moscow and Teheran prior to 1979, the USSR was pleased when the US lost its regional policeman and listening post on the Soviet border. Moreover, despite Soviet reservations regarding Khomeini's Islamic vision, the anti-American flavor of the revolution in Teheran appeared to provide the means to establish a congruence of interests which could be translated into significant political and military advantage. After all, the economic basis for extensive relations had been laid under the Shah.

At first, it appeared as if the Soviets' job would be easy: The seizure of American diplomatic personnel in Teheran signalled to Moscow that a major opportunity awaited. Initial press reports of the hostage crisis were exceptionally low key. Dispatches indicated that the students who occupied the embassy found documents showing US complicity in Iranian affairs. When Washington froze Iranian assets in this country, the Soviet press claimed that the US was using force against Iran. In the initial phases of the crisis, Soviet Farsi broadcasts beamed at Iran contained particularly strident anti-American commentaries. Following protests from Washington, the tone of the radio programs was softened. As the crisis continued, each US action was met with charges from *Pravda* or other press organs that the US sought to increase the tensions inherent in the crisis. Few reporters mentioned the illegality of the seizure itself. In fact, the official Soviet line was openly sympathetic to Teheran. As a correspondent wrote in *Pravda:*

> To be sure, the seizure of the American embassy in and of itself does not conform to the international convention concerning respect for diplomatic privileges and immunity. However, one cannot pull this act out of the overall context of American–Iranian relations.[4]

By the same token, the Soviets did have a long-standing relationship—albeit an uneasy one—with Iraq. Baghdad, despite its 1972 Friendship and Cooperation Treaty with the USSR, had proven somewhat troublesome. Indeed from the mid-seventies on, Iraq's independence included diversifying its arms supply, execution of the Iraqi Communist Party leadership, and condemnation of the Afghan invasion. For Moscow, these issues seemingly outweighed the Iraqi role in the Arab opposition to Camp David. Nonetheless, as the Soviets were to find out, there were limits to the estrangement. The USSR, therefore, conducted its policy after September 1980 with an eye toward the impact that policy would have on bilateral relations with each of the combatants.

Soviet policy toward the Iran–Iraq War provides the central focus of this study. Yet, the impact of the Islamic revolution on Soviet calculations could not be ignored. Therefore, Chapter One discusses Soviet interpretations of the Iranian revolution and evaluations of the potent impact of the fundamentalist revival for Moscow's clients in the region.

Chapters Two, Three, and Four examine the Iran–Iraq War. The conflict creates problems for Moscow in three ways. As already noted, as long as the state of war continues, it will affect the USSR's ties with Iran and Iraq. Publicly, the Kremlin maintained a stance of strict neutrality. It was obviously calculated that public/official neutrality could not further damage the already attenuated ties with Iraq and might avoid alienating the Islamic regime in Teheran. This is not to say that the state of bilateral ties depended solely on the war. As will be seen, the Moscow–Teheran and the Moscow–Baghdad relationship each contained a dynamic of its own, although the war certainly affected Soviet fortunes.

Equally important to Moscow were the ramifications of the war for the superpower balance in the region. Moscow, with a view to maintaining the gains that the Iranian revolution had produced, wanted also to prevent a renewal of Iranian–American ties. The leadership clearly feared that aid to or support for Iraq would push Teheran back into Washington's arms. Moreover, the US, faced with Soviet troops in Afghanistan and the war, moved to protect what it saw as its legitimate interests in the region. The US beefed up its naval presence there and, more recently, providing escort to reflagged Kuwaiti oil tankers. Hence, Moscow's perceptions of American diplomatic and military policy and US reaction to events in the Gulf played a significant part in Soviet calculations. Finally, the war has been detrimental to Soviet policy objectives in the rest of the Middle East because it has caused significant realignments in the Arab world and deflected Arab attention from the Arab–Israeli–Palestinian nexus. Thus, given the constraints of regional and superpower politics, the Gulf War offered Moscow no easy choices.

Mikhail Gorbachev inherited these problems when he acceded to power in March 1985. At that time, the Gulf War was already four-and-one-half years old and the policy dilemmas it created readily apparent. At the same time, Gorbachev had his own priorities and individual style which differed markedly from those of his predecessors. The new Soviet leader came to power intent on revitalizing the ailing Soviet economy, while in the foreign policy sphere he indicated a new flexibility. This study will explore, as well, therefore, the impact that Mikhail Gorbachev has had on Soviet policy toward the Gulf.

Notes

1. "Agreement between Russian Socialist Federal Soviet Republic and Persia," dated February 21, 1921, included in *Dokumenty vneshnei politiki SSSR* (Moscow: Ministry of Foreign Affairs, 1959), pp. 536–537.

2. For a full account of the events leading up to the invasion and an analysis of the reasons for the invasion, see Henry S. Bradsher, *Afghanistan and the Soviet Union* (Durham, N.C.: Duke University Press, 1983).

3. Cited in Benjamin F. Schemmer, "Was the US Ready to Resort to Nuclear Weapons for the Persian Gulf in the 1980s," *Armed Forces Journal International,* September 1986, p. 92.

4. A. Petrov, "Display Prudence and Restraint," *Pravda,* December 5, 1979, p. 5, in *Current Digest of the Soviet Press,* Vol. 31, No. 49, January 2, 1980, p. 26.

1

Soviet Perspectives on Islam as a Third World Political Force

Islam as a potent political force is a relatively new item on the international agenda; yet for the Soviet Union, Islam has long been an issue. As early as 1917, Lenin addressed the "Toiling Muslim Peoples of the East," and in 1918 the new Soviet government established a Commissariat on Muslim Affairs. In the early 1920s, the Bolshevik government negotiated treaties with Iran, Turkey, and Afghanistan—its first with any Third World countries. Moscow has, since then, maintained a consistent interest in the contiguous Muslim countries, and in the post-World War II period the USSR established a very large stake in the Middle East–Gulf region. Despite the USSR's active role in the region as armorer and mentor to the Arabs, prior to the late seventies, the question of Islam as a factor in international relations was assiduously downplayed.

Beginning in 1979, events in Iran and Afghanistan thrust the Islamic question into the decision-making calculus of the Politburo. Suddenly, political problems with Islamic components could be found throughout the Middle East: the tribal and ethnic nature of the rebellion in Afghanistan that precipitated the introduction of Soviet troops; the creation of an Islamic republic in Iran that turned out to be anti-American and anti-Soviet; the outbreak of the Gulf War between Shi'i Iran and Sunni-led Iraq that undermined Soviet plans for a united anti-Israel, anti-American front; the assassination of Anwar Sadat by an Islamic group; and the activization of the Muslim Brotherhood in Syria that clearly threatened the regime of a pro-Soviet Middle East ally. And this is by no means an exhaustive list.

An earlier version of this article appeared in Paul Marantz and Blema Steinberg, eds., *Superpower Involvement in the Middle East* (Boulder: Westview Press, 1985). The author would like to thank David E. Powell for his comments on an earlier draft.

Faced with a phenomenon that obviously affected foreign policy calculations (and perhaps domestic policy as well), Soviet officials and academics set out to investigate and explain the Islamic revival and to assess its political impact. Although Soviet Islamic studies, as conducted by anthropologists, historians, and philosophers are not new, the resurgence of Islam as a political force since 1979 galvanized the academic community. As early as 1980–1981, one can find within the literature calls for research on Islam. And, unlike earlier studies, this work was to be conducted by economists and political scientists with long-term Middle East experience and expertise. The Institute of Oriental Studies became the center of Islamic studies, sponsoring several working groups on ideological trends in the "East." According to a report detailing works in progress that appeared in *Narody Azii i Afriki,* events established the Islamic resurgence as the top research priority. Among the topics to be investigated were traditional religious ideologies, the doctrine of "Islamic economics" (especially as practiced in Pakistan), and the "Islamic state."[1]

Soviet analyses and perspectives on Islam may be found as well in official pronouncements, press reports, and editorials. The official statements and academic works are linked by the close ties between the institutes of the Soviet Academy of Sciences and the policy-making world. First, academics not infrequently wear two hats. Not only are they researchers or professors within the institutes, but several are also members of the Central Committee's International Department. Second, while we cannot necessarily link the views of specific academics with those of the late Yuri Andropov, Konstantin Chernenko, or Mikhail Gorbachev, or their colleagues in the Politburo, we can infer that the debates occurring on the pages of scholarly journals or between institutes reflect unresolved political questions.

In the view of many Western observers, general research areas are delineated by party higher-ups. Yet, other analysts argue that Soviet scholars do initiate a certain number of research projects themselves. It would seem probable that, to some extent, both assessments are accurate. While some flexibility may exist in choosing topics, research within the social science institutes of the Academy of Sciences is responsive to party needs. In fact, the topics are frequently those on which policy-makers request assessents.[2] Whether to elaborate on Soviet foreign policy decisions or because the bureaucrats need specific information, the institutes dealing with contemporary issues are instructed to delve into timely research topics. Academics are called upon to do research, as the Soviets put it, "in light" of party congress decisions, and there is evidence to indicate that internal working papers may be passed on to party officials. The new specialists on Islam openly acknowledged the link between their research projects and policy. One orientalist went so far as to admit that these presumably accurate assessments of political Islam would aid the Soviet propaganda effort.[3] In this era of *glasnost'*, the parameters of public debate are certainly more wide-ranging. The pages of both popular and academic journals openly question past foreign policy decisions. Nonetheless, the general "rules" outlined above still seem to hold true. What has increased is the consultation among specialists from the several foreign policy related think tanks, the International Department, and the foreign ministry.[4]

This chapter will focus on Soviet perspectives on the international aspects of the Islamic question. The first section will explore how Soviet pronouncements and writings about political Islam fit into the general Soviet understanding of political processes in the Third World. The next section will focus on the impact of the Iranian revolution. Although there are other manifestations of the Islamic revival, Iran has been the major focus of Soviet Islamic studies because it is the single case of a continuing self-proclaimed Islamic revolution. We will also look at overall Soviet assessments of the Islamic phenomenon. This analysis will include attempts to answer the following questions: Why has there been an Islamic "awakening"? And, how does it fit with Soviet theories of "progressive" development? Finally, we will look at the implications for Soviet perspectives and policy posed by recent events: Can the USSR cultivate long-term relations with Islamic countries or will post-Khomeini Islam be a major obstacle to Soviet policy?

Soviet Third World Studies and Islam

Academic and official analyses and interpretations of the so-called Islamic revolution must be understood within the context of Soviet studies of Third World political processes. These studies, or *vostoko-vedenie,* were spurred by Moscow's increasing involvement in the Third World and reflect Soviet experiences there. In general, Soviet studies of the Third World reveal the analytical categories observers used to judge events and trends in this unstable terrain and which, therefore, underlie Soviet assessments of problems and prospects. The several analytical frameworks adopted by Soviet academics have proven to be a combination of Marxist–Leninist rhetoric and social science and of increasingly sophisticated studies of the trends and dynamics of the Third World.

As the USSR's ties to Third World countries proliferated, Moscow had to create a fit between its professed ideology and its actual foreign policy. This process was complicated by the emergence in the sixties of Third World leaders who espoused vehement anti-Westernism and proclaimed themselves socialist. Although the Soviets welcomed their anti-Westernism and even praised many of their domestic programs, these same leaders jailed and sometimes executed local communist party members. Thus, Soviet politicians and academics had to work out criteria to determine the "acceptability" of allies. The resulting criteria, in almost every case, were based upon a pro-Soviet foreign policy combined with radical domestic programs including an acceptable ideological base.

In the early sixties, scholars elaborated the Noncapitalist Path (NCP) which, as the name implies, was a "path" or direction from underdevelopment to socialism bypassing the capitalist stage of development. It included prescriptions intended to answer the problems of underdevelopment with programs designed to create pro-Soviet allies. As a measure of "acceptability," incremental steps along the NCP were considered "progressive." However, between 1965 and 1968 several pro-Soviet radicals who were said to be leading their states on the NCP were toppled by coups. These losses jolted the Kremlin leaders and Soviet academics into the realization that the noncapitalist construct was insufficient. It did not address the realities of Third World politics or provide an adequate measure of the reliability or longevity of Soviet friends. Under the guise of creative Marxism, scholars adopted newer categories, some of which were intended as models of developing societies, while others combined more realistic data collection with the never-abandoned socialist blueprint. Academics and party officials alike began to refer to "States of Socialist Orientation." The construct, first adopted in the mid- to late seventies, responded to the advent of Third World radicals who proclaim themselves Marxist–Leninist. A socialist-oriented state is more orthodox than earlier noncapitalist states, and the list of countries fitting the category is much shorter. (Among the socialist-oriented states are Angola, Ethiopia, Mozambique, and South Yemen.) Most of the programmatic recommendations remain, but the newer prescriptions were designed to institutionalize pro-Soviet orientations. Observers devoted additional attention to political institutions and methods that they hoped would ensure the tenure in power of pro-Soviet leaders.[5]

All of the modifictions introduced into Soviet development literature over the last twenty-plus years seemed designed to generate more accurate pictures of the politics and problems in Third World countries. They have included questions related to the political cultures and ideological development in those states in which the USSR has a military, economic, and diplomatic stake. Many of these countries in which the Kremlin hopes to institutionalize a pro-Soviet foreign policy have significant Muslim populations. In some, Islam is the proclaimed state religion; in others, various brands of "progressive" quasi-socialist development strategies are infused with references to traditional Islamic culture.

In the sixties, when optimism about Third World political change was greatest, Soviet scholars evidenced a striking ambivalence regarding Third World ideologies and socialism. They condemned African socialism as unscientific, un-"progressive," and in some cases dangerous. Simultaneously, the Middle Eastern varieties of Arab or Islamic socialism were handled differently. Ironically, the early Soviet development literatuare glossed over Islam. Although the emphasis on Islamic traditions in Egypt or Algeria, for example, was subject to periodic criticism, the Soviets recognized early on that Islam was useful in the then burgeoning anti-colonial struggle. (Islam became part of the nationalist rhetoric in many Middle Eastern and North African states and was, therefore, seen as anti-Western.) Hence, the criticisms were never as stinging as those reserved for African socialism.

The use of Egypt and Algeria as examples is no accident. Both at the time were portrayed as "progressive" states on the Noncapitalist Path; moreover, Algeria, as we shall see below, is held up today as an example of an "acceptable" Islamic state. A history of Soviet evaluations of either Algerian or Egyptian political developments is beyond the scope of this work, but several points need to be made. While Soviet orientalists took note of increasing nationalist fervor in Algeria prior to the outbreak of the Algerian war on November 1, 1954, they were definitely discomfited by the strength of Islamic elements within the nationalist movement. When open revolt against French authorities finally began, Soviet observers sided with the nationalists despite the Front de liberation national's (FLN) declaration that its goal was the creation of a democratic and social government in agreement with the principles of Islam. Then, in 1962, when Algeria was declared independent, the FLN leadership drafted what came to be called the Tripoli Program, outlining Algeria's socialist future. Again, several observers took exception to the emphasis placed on Algeria's Islamic heritage. By 1964, when Algerian President Ahmed Ben Bella seemed a secure Soviet ally, criticism of the Islamic factor softened. V. Kudriavtsev, *Izvestiia's* political commentator, stated that one must take into account the strength of the state's Islamic heritage in building a society based on socialist underpinnings.[6]

In the Egyptian case, ideological and religious issues surfaced briefly in 1962, but were glossed over in the generally positive appraisals of Nasir's Egypt. When in 1962 the Nasir government issued the Charter of National Action which was supposed to outline Egyptian socialist development, Soviet orientalists praised the document because it referred to scientific socialism. Yet, the charter also reaffirmed the religious nature of Egyptian society. In a *Pravda* interview given at approximately the same time, the Egyptian president underscored his view that Islam was the religion of socialism. The *Pravda* correspondent, V. Mayevskii, concluded that precisely because of its Islamic component, the charter reflected "contradictions existing in the social development" of Egypt.[7]

This muted criticism of Islam did not interfere with Soviet relations with either country nor did it prevent positive if not glowing appraisals of both countries' "progressive" development. Pragmatic politics dictated that Islam as a political and cultural issue be downplayed, if not ignored. If anything, Soviet observers seconded the anti-imperialist aspects of many Islamic-nationalist pronouncements. Fifteen years later, Islam emerged as a new and powerful Middle East force. Fundamentalism, as it came to be called in the West, affected politics both within and among states. In contrast to the earlier period, the Islamic revival could not be ignored. The course of the Iranian revolution and its repercussions in all Muslim states demonstrated that Islam could affect—in some cases adversely—Soviet foreign policy calculations.

The Impact of Iran

The Iranian revolution under the leadership of the Shi'i clergy appears to have surprised the Soviet leadership as much as their Western counterparts. The Soviet press covered the turmoil in Iran, but no observers anticipated the rapid collapse of the Peacock Throne. Because the USSR and Iran enjoyed mutually beneficial economic relations, it would seem fair to state that the Soviets were relatively well satisfied with the *status quo*. Therefore, the advent of the Islamic regime in Teheran raised a host of questions for Soviet (and Western) observers. Why was the Shah overthrown? What was the role of the Shi'i clergy? What happened to leftist forces within the country? And finally, at what point did the revolution evolve into a theocratic dictatorship? Initially, only the first two questions were posed; however, as the clergy instituted the Islamic republic and turned increasingly anti-democratic, Soviet orientalists delved into the questions regarding the long-term course of the Islamic revolution.

In the period following the Shah's exit from Iran, Moscow was optimistic concerning the future of the Iranian revolution. *Pravda*'s political commentator stressed that the collapse of the monarchy created the favorable preconditions for the end of imperialist domination and for the "democratization" of the country, *i.e.,* the participation of leftist (including communist) forces.[8] Most importantly, orientalists had to explain the key role of the clergy and Islam's revolutionary political potential. From the outset, most Soviet observers concluded that repressive conditions in Iran precluded the rise to leadership of groups other than the clergy. Calling Islam a "catalyst of nationalist attitudes," Soviet observers at the time went so far as to claim that the Iranian revolution was in no way a religious movement despite the active participation of Shi'i clergy.[9]

Soviet optimism continued throughout 1979, despite ethnic uprisings and intensifying political factionalism that complicated the process of regime consolidation. At this time, Moscow gave relatively high marks to the Iranian revolution. For example, as part of its May Day celebrations, the Soviet leadership sent "warm greetings to the Iranian people who have carried out an anti-imperialist national liberation revolution."[10] With hindsight, it would seem that Soviet observers were naive about the potency of Islam as an ideology and about the political power of the clergy. What does seem clear is that these optimistic pronouncements reflected the hopes the Kremlin placed on the Ayatollah's anti-Americanism.

By the same token, Soviet academics and journalists kept an eye on the consolidation process and presented detailed accounts of the problems confronting the Ayatollah Khomeini. As the revolution unfolded, the Soviet leadership watched uneasily as revolutionary factions fought for political position. Expressing concern about the lack of unity among the now victorious anti-Shah forces, several writers took note of the growing dispute between religious and secular revolutionary participants. While most writers were careful not to alienate the Khomeini forces, one did allege that the clergy "used" the peoples' movement.[11] In contrast, the majority argued at this time that socialism was not counterposed to Islam. The weekly, *New Times,* added in a prescriptive vein:

> If the revolution, which is not only Islamic but also national democratic, is to preserve its social content and progressive character . . . it must rely on a single front which besides the Islamic and democratic tendencies should contain an element of Marxism.[12]

What the Soviets were proposing was a coalition government which would include Tudeh (communist) Party participation.

Yet, in contrast to Soviet hopes, it became increasingly clear that nonreligious forces were being suppressed. Consequently, Soviet experts took note of the changing political tenor of the revolution. Their later assessments focused on the stages of the revolution, the class forces involved at particular stages, and the role of the clergy. Soviet observers concurred that at each succeeding phase of the revolution, various groups opposed to the clergy were weeded out, ultimately including radicals and the Tudeh Party. Moreover, the clergy, seeking to protect its own interests, endeavored to institutionalize Islamic principles and ideals.[13] By 1982, Soviet observers evidenced genuine contempt for Khomeini and his programs. Commentators claimed that Khomeini's social programs reminded them of the Middle Ages, while several journalists charged that the clergy gave priority to establishing their own monopoly on power rather than to solving pressing socioeconomic problems.

With the arrest and trial of Tudeh Party members in early 1983 and the expulsion of Soviet diplomats in May of that year, the Soviets resorted to outright name-calling. For example, Vladimir Volinskii, an Iranian specialist whose radio programs to Iran were initiated in 1982 to "clear up misconceptions," criticized Khomeini's drive to become the arbiter of all Middle East revolutions. He said: "Islam has been declared as the only and most revolutionary teaching and this propaganda has reached the point of buffoonery."[14] Still other observers claimed that Khomeini and the clergy had, in effect, perverted the course of the revolution. As one journalist said: "The tyranny under which Iranians are suffering has not been lessened yet. . . . In present day Iran those who want to cut short the hands of the exploiters and safeguard the Islamic revolution are branded as criminals. . . ."[15] R. A. Ul'ianovskii, a prominent orientalist and then deputy director of the International Department, offered perhaps the final word. Claiming that religion is a primitive form of social awareness and that the Shi'i clergy have instituted religious despotism, he added:

> [the clergy used only] that part of these traditions which was reflected in the conservative, and at times reactionary, dogmas of Islam struggling mainly to perpetuate the conditions of its existence and consolidate its political hegemony. . . . The clergy . . . did everything in its power to establish the *outdated* moral and ethical standards of the Koran and the Shari'a. . . .[16]

Thus far, the Islamic regime in Teheran has survived its own political struggles, the Iraqi attack, and international ostracism. With the hindsight of several years, Soviet experts renewed their interest in the early days of the revolution. This time, however, they sought to explain the failure of leftist forces within the country and the consequent establishment of what they recognized as a theocratic dictatorship. Gone were the naive pronouncements about the role of the Shi'i clergy. In their stead, we find detailed "classical" Marxist–Leninist analyses of the class leanings of the clergy and those other groups with which they were aligned. The current interpretation is that the clergy itself was divided between those who sought to protect their holdings from the Shah's White Revolution and those without property who were connected to the masses. The two groups had a sometimes antagonistic, sometimes cooperative relationship. Indeed, it has been put forward that Khomeini did not achieve unquestioned ideological dominance for the first two years.

Of course, the proverbial other side of the coin is the question of what happened to the Fedayin, Mujaheedin, and the Tudeh. Soviet orientalists devoted many pages to examinations of the ideological content of their respective platforms. What is more significant for our purposes is the conclusion that the lack of unity among these leftist forces prevented concerted action as a counterveiling pressure against theocratic tendencies. Not only were there disagreements among these groups, but there were also no institutional linkages to facilitate discussion and action. According to orientalists, under these circumstances, the revolution acquired a capitalist bent by 1982.[17]

Clearly, none of these theories denies the power and influence of Islam in the Iranian context. Many of these same authors allege that in the earliest days of the turmoil, the sway of the clergy prevented the liberals from establishing a constitutional democracy. And in the final analysis, the experts were forced to conclude that the peculiarities of the Iranian revolution—especially its intensity—were directly derived from Islam.[18]

Whether or not the Islamic revolution will survive the death of Khomeini remains to be seen. Whatever the current interpretation of the Iranian revolution, Khomeini-ism as a force has had a definite impact on other Muslim states. The spread of political Islam prompted Soviet Third World specialists to develop more general explanations of the Islamic resurgence and to evaluate its political impact. These interpretations of Islamic revivalism have changed less over the years than the analyses of the revolution from which it is derived.

According to the general Soviet argument, and echoing some of the earlier Soviet pronouncements, the Islamic resurgence comprises an important element in the total liberation process. Soviet observers explained that the less-developed countries are supposed to choose from competing development strategies. Yet, from the Soviet perspective, Iran demonstrated both that Western models are unsuited to transitional societies and that Iran and other states have rejected Western models of development. One leading scholar in the field of Islamic studies wrote that the Iranian revolution "proves that Western models of modernization are unacceptable for transitional multistructural societies [*i.e.,* the LDC's]."[19] According to this line of reasoning it is precisely the penetration of alien Western models of modernization that triggers the politicization of the Islamic masses.[20]

In a corollary, Moscow sees Islam as a useful tool which complements the traditional communist emphasis on mass mobilization. As one Soviet writer put it:

> the disillusionment of the politically active forces . . . in Western models of political struggle, the inclusion of the middle class in national liberation movements, the anti-Arab position of the West with regard to the Palestinian problem . . . led nationalists to [use] Islam as an instrument of the masses.[21]

Moreover, scholars concluded that Islam becomes political all the more easily because the masses see in its dogma the rejection of inequality and injustice.[22]

The authors of an important article which appeared in *Mirovaia ekonomika i mezhdunarodnye otnosheniia* went beyond the rejection of Western ideals to explain the Islamic revival. They listed dissatisfaction with inflation, the ideological vacuum existing in the nonindustrial states, and the consequent search for an Islamic alternative.[23] The thrust of all these analyses is that Islam is obviously a "useful" anti-Western force. As Brezhnev said in his speech at the twenty-sixth CPSU congress in 1981:

> Despite its [the Iranian revolution's] complex and contradictory nature, it is basically an anti-imperialist revolution although domestic and foreign reaction is seeking to alter this character. . . .
>
> The Iranian people are seeking their own path to freedom and prosperity. We sincerely wish them success and we are prepared to develop good relations with Iran. . . .
>
> We communists respect the religious convictions of the people who profess Islam and any other religion. . . . The liberation struggle may develop under the banner of Islam.[24]

Later analyses carry this theme forward, but in a more sophisticated fashion. Viewing Islam as a kind of cultural nationalism, scholars asserted that what might be called the "Iranianization" of political and cultural thought led to Islamicization. According to one review article, Iranian thinkers rejected alien Western ideals and substituted Islam which was seen as a universal social doctrine in which Iran could occupy a unique place.[25]

Soviet observers have clearly been attracted to that part of Islamic ideologies which is anti-Western. Yet as the above examination of events in Iran showed, there is as well an "anti-progressive" element in it that is unhealthy for socialist forces in any given country. There is thus within Soviet writings about Islam a distinct ambivalence. Many concluded that despite its anti-Westernism, which makes the Islamic revolution to some degree "progressive," its "reactionary" elements are equally strong.

In their attempts to determine Islam's political thrust, scholars also investigated traditional Islamic views on questions of justice and equality, as well as on so-called Islamic economic models. Several orientalists claimed that Islam was anti-equalitarian; yet, these and other scholars stated at the same time that the masses were drawn to its promise of social justice. Because traditional Islamic society had very specific economic rules and because the Marxist–Leninist prism dictates a major concern with economics, it seems natural that a segment of the Soviet academic community devote its energies to studying proposals for Islamic economic systems in the Muslim Third World. A survey of the literature reveals an increasing number of articles detailing Islamic-style international economics and Islamic banks. Major differences of opinion exist on these issues as well. Certain scholars have focused on the so-called Islamic economic system as implemented by the late President Zia al Haq of Pakistan. Indeed, they see the system as completely "reactionary" and condemn Zia for using Islam to further the cause of reactionary Muslim countries such as Saudi Arabia.[26] According to a long analysis in *Nauka i religiia,* even so-called Islamic socialist ideals are in reality merely fronts for bourgeois forces. The author of this article charged further that reactionary (anti-Soviet) forces want to "ensure that the only thing remaining of Islam is religious zeal bordering on fanaticism which can be turned against the national liberation struggle."[27]

By the same token, other scholars see positive potential in these constructs—again, insofar as they are anti-Western. Evgenii Primakov, currently director of the Institute of World Economics and International Affairs of the Soviet Academy of Sciences and a long-time Middle East hand, concluded that the "Islamic development strategy would work only insofar as it is based on leftist forces and the mobilization of the workers."[28] More recent investigations see not so much the ambiguous nature of Islam, but the differentiation of the Islamic movement into leftists and fundamentalists. The former contains those who are anti-colonial and anti-Zionist. The latter include those who, while anti-

Western, are anti-socialist. Additionally, fundamentalist groups are, to the Kremlin's dismay, anti-Soviet.

The Implications for Policy

What do these assessments mean for Soviet foreign policy? Observers, to underscore the obvious, recognize that the Islamic revolution affects more than just the domestic politics of any given Muslim state; it has altered relations among Middle East states as well. Thus, the international aspects of the phenomenon may well have a significant impact not only on Soviet bilateral relations, but also on regional objectives and calculations.

The record of Soviet involvement in the Third World suggests that Moscow's activities are guided by geopolitical considerations (*i.e.,* concern for ports and strategic access) and by the desire to counter Western (and Chinese) influence positions. Both motivations are of major consequence in the Middle East where the Soviets have sought a naval presence and acted to reinforce the anti-Western attitudes of many of the region's leaders. Another apparent Soviet goal in the Third World is the establishment of diplomatic relations with as many states as possible. Moscow sees the proliferation of its state-to-state diplomatic ties as a symbol of its acceptance as an international actor and as a superpower. A corollary goal is to cultivate friends who will help achieve these various objectives. Cultivation, as a foreign policy goal, means convincing Third World elites that a genuine coincidence of interests exists between them and the USSR. Moreover, Soviet propagandists seem to feel that pro-Soviet orientations will thrive best where common issues dominate the political rhetoric. Observers expect their socialist heirs in the Third World to devote resources to political education and indoctrination. Yet, scholars also recognize that what one specialist called the "backwardness of the masses" will prevent the adoption of scientific socialism. The label "backward" seems to refer to ethnic and tribal identifications as well as to religious ideologies including Islam. Most of these were seen as naive, at best.

Interestingly, although the Soviets have exhibited some sensitivity to the potential contagion of political Islam, the very existence of a sizeable Muslim population within the USSR may facilitate the cultivation effort. Since the revolution in Iran and the near-collapse of the Marxist regime in Afghanistan, innumerable Soviet journals and foreign language broadcasts have been devoted to Muslim life within the Soviet Union. The effort to depict Muslim life positively may be considered a significant part of the Soviet propaganda drive to allay fears among the Arab and Gulf states of Moscow's hostility to Islamic principles.

In fact, Soviet Muslim delegations frequently meet with coreligionists from the Arab world and the Soviet press contains references to the "international relations" of Soviet Muslims. In October 1986, for example, the USSR hosted what was billed as an international Islamic conference. Participants included Soviet Muslim dignitaries as well as foreign journalists and representatives from some Middle Eastern states. The Baku meeting represented a major propaganda offensive. It was reported in international broadcasts beamed at the Middle East and in journals with international distribution. Moreover, its agenda differed significantly from that of the Islamic Conference Organization. Its themes were peace and nuclear disarmament and not the Iran–Iraq War. Ultimately, the convening of the conference indicates the continuing recognition of Islam as a major international force.

However, the record of Soviet–Third World relations also illustrates that despite these efforts and despite Soviet attempts to achieve influence over Third World friends by distributing economic and military assistance, the best Moscow may be able to achieve is a coincidence of interests. With a small number of exceptions, formal alliances are few. Even in those cases in which friendship and cooperation treaties have been signed, serious policy disagreements have, on more than one occasion, disrupted relations. Therefore, the key question then becomes how strong and long-lived that congruence of interests may be.

Islamic Solidarity

As with the question of the domestic uses of Islam, questions of Islamic solidarity and Islamic unity were downplayed until very recently. What little comment there was tended, in a prescriptive vein, to discourage unification schemes. For example, one long-term Soviet objective in the Middle East was the creation of a united anti-Israel, anti-American front composed of Gulf and Middle East states under Soviet leadership. Thus far the Soviets have been unable to put together such a coalition, however. Islamic affiliations transcend left–right politics. Moreover, from the Soviet perspective, Islamic ties may put Syria and Libya in the same camp as Saudi Arabia thus forming an exclusive club for which Moscow's membership credentials are not terribly strong, and its hoped-for leadership position even weaker.

Generally, the evidence indicates that Moscow is discomfited by calls for Islamic solidarity whether emanating from the Islamic Conference or from Iran and Iraq as each pursued its military objectives in the Gulf War. For example, the commentator on a domestic television program, "The World Today," noted:

Some circles in Teheran call today for the continuation of the war in order to punish the Iraqi leaders and to spread the Iranian type of Islam. Are these countries not paying too high a price in trying to clarify with the aid of military operations the point of who is better the Sunnis or the Shi'ites?[29]

With the resurgence of political Islam, the Islamic Conference as an international governmental organization has acquired major significance. As a result, for the first time several articles detailing the workings of the organization and most importantly its international positions have appeared in the major Soviet foreign policy journals. As might be expected, Soviet observers approve of the organization insofar as its orientation is pro-Palestinian, anti-Israel, and anti-American. Nonetheless, these same commentators take issue with its composition. They accuse the conference of being unduly influenced by "rich conservative Muslim states" which permit the "reactionary uses of Islam" by imperialists. In particular, the Soviets are unhappy that the conference has discussed the situation of Muslims in the USSR and the fighting in Afghanistan. In fact, the Islamic Conference suspended Afghanistan's membership following the 1979 Soviet invasion. Thus, despite the conference's agreement with some Soviet policies, it is still distinctly anti-communist. Moreover, it would seem fair to conclude that Moscow's line would be even harsher were not several Soviet friends members of the conference.

Recently, Moscow has evidenced a more differentiated approach to the ICO. Soviet writers have lavished praise on the Al Quds, Jerusalem, committee of the organization and on the consistent support given to an international conference on the Middle East. These same observers had difficulty, in contrast, when the ICO voted in 1984 to readmit Egypt. While downplaying the end of Egypt's isolation, experts were pleased when the ICO strongly condemned US policies toward members Syria and Libya. Finally, the Soviets have clearly recognized that the organization cannot be ignored. In fact, the USSR sent formal official greetings to the 1987 meeting in Kuwait.

Afghanistan

No discussion of Soviet attitudes toward Islam would ·be complete without mention of Afghanistan. Although Islam was not the major precipitating factor of the Christmastime invasion, the tribal population's depth of Islamic feeling and resentment of the Kabul regime's policies hampered Soviet efforts to stabilize the situation. Over the years, the USSR maintained a strong interest in its mountainous neighbor, including a 1921 treaty, military intervention in 1929, and economic and military agreements beginning in the early fifties. The Soviet stake in Afghanistan increased significantly in the period between the overthrow of the monarchy in 1973 and the April 1978 coup which brought the local communist party to power. Once a Marxist-Leninist regime came to power in Kabul, the Soviets intensified their involvement. By the fall of 1979, despite close ties with the Soviet Union (including a Friendship and Cooperation Treaty), the communist regime, threatened by political infighting and by intensifying attacks by Islamic tribal insurgents, was on the verge of collapse. The Soviet Union apparently decided that only armed intervention could save the regime to which its prestige was now linked.

To judge from public pronouncements regarding Afghanistan, the Soviets blame Hafizullah Amin for much of their current difficulties. They accuse him of initiating ill-timed, radical reforms without regard to the Islamic sentiments of the local population. One report, for example, describes how a representative of the revolutionary committee would arrive in a village to redistribute land only to be followed by a local *mullah* who would proclaim that Allah did not permit seizing another's land. The report continued: "This is the reality of the situation. To be sure, it does not mean that land reform in Afghanistan is intrinsically unsuitable. But it did turn out that the initial land distribution was extremist, ill-conceived, and unsuitable in specific conditions.[30]

As a result, Soviet propaganda stressed that the Karmal regime understood the Islamic underpinnings of Afghan society. An Afghan official, writing in *Partiinaia zhizn'* stated:

[Every effort is being made to] see that the ideals and goals of the April revolution would be correctly and deeply understood by faithful Muslims and by all laborers. . . . Considering that most of the country's population practices Islam, the [party] clearly and distinctly formulates its principled policy in relation to this religion. The revolution is a response to the aspirations and hopes of the laboring Muslims of the country.[31]

This theme has been echoed in broadcasts to Iran as well. A Farsi broadcast claimed that Islam would be taken into account when the Kabul government initiated new revolutionary programs. Moscow announced that the Karmal regime created a Muslim affairs department, restored local mosques, and permitted the celebration of Muslim holidays. But Radio Moscow in Farsi also underscored that tolerance did not include the active proselytizing of reactionary clergy who "eulogize" the Afghan monarchy.[32] Implicitly, the Kremlin pointed out the possibility of a compromise between pro-Marxist programs and respect for the Islamic heritage of the many Middle East countries. In addition, a broadcast such as the one mentioned above has significant propaganda value. The USSR is clearly attempting not only to appease local Muslims and their counterparts in the rest of the region, but also to placate the Khomeini regime.

Soviet experiences in Afghanistan and Iran coupled with the problems that Soviet clients have faced with Islamic movements have convinced academics and policymakers alike that the strength of Islamic sentiment may indeed be an obstacle to Soviet Middle East objectives. That Kremlin policymakers are unhappy with this turn of events is obvious; but it is also clear that they recognize the need to come to terms with it. As was noted above, the thrust of current Soviet writings on the Third World is to suggest methods for consolidating power and maintaining pro-Soviet leaders in office. Consequently, the prescriptions now offered by Soviet Third World specialists include the need to blend tradition and modernity. Scholars and Kremlin politicians have come to the conclusion, albeit belatedly, that it is a mistake for local leadership to ignore the diverse religious, ethnic, and historical traditions of the LDCs. Instead, they call for a compromise between the old (Islam) and the new (socialist orientation).

The journal *Nauka i religiia* argued, for example, that several states had achieved just such a compromise:

In countries of socialist orientation the governing revolutionary democrats take into account the religious character of the ideology of the masses . . . showing them that these reforms are not in conflict with the spirit of Islam. In the PDRY [South Yemen] for example, scientific socialism has become the official ideological platform of the national democratic revolution.[33]

Whether or not such a synthesis can succeed is still being debated within the foreign policy institutes. Although orientalists hope that the Islamic socialist ideologies of "progressive" leaders will evolve into full-fledged Marxism-Leninism, they also caution that bourgeois ideologues will use so-called Islamic socialism for their own ends.[34] And as was noted above, Evgenii Primakov argued that Islam could safely comprise part of a "progressive" ideology only if pro-Soviet, leftist elements are firmly in power. Nodari Simoniia, a Soviet expert on the Third World known for his cautious assessments, went even further. In a roundtable discussion he argued forcibly that the synthesis—that is of Islamic or other brands of socialism—alone will not ensure "progress." At some point, a "revolutionary shift" in power must take place. For Simoniia, pro-Soviet orientations can be achieved only by the accession to power of Marxist elements (if not a full-fledged vanguard party).[35]

These academic assessments reflect the Kremlin's desire to work with Islamic states and "progressive" Islamic forces, but most probably when Islam is not used as an end in itself. A Khomeini-type leader who seeks to implement an Iranian style revolution is not, therefore, a likely Soviet ally. This is not to say, however, that Moscow would rule out dealing with the Khomeini regime or its successor. Indeed, as will be seen in subsequent chapters, the Kremlin worked hard in 1987 to reestablish an on-going economic relationship such as existed prior to the revolution.

But, an anti-Western "progressive" leader who nonetheless uses Islamic slogans would seem not only a target for cultivation, but also a potential Soviet friend. Moreover, the Kremlin appears to recognize that political Islam has acquired such momentum in the Middle East that no ruler can afford to ignore it. In the published proceedings of a conference of orientalists held in Tbilisi, it was noted that many contemporary Third World leaders see Islam as a "constituent part and key lever in the realization of their political and economic programs."[36] Given the emphasis on the consolidation of power and given the potency of political Islam, the prescription appears to be that a compromise must be worked out and that implicitly Islam should be used as a mobilizing and legitimating force wherever possible.

In this regard, it is interesting to note that Soviet Third World specialists are restudying the Algerian experience. The late President Houari Boumedienne and current Algerian leader Chadli Benjedid are lauded by Moscow for their use of Islam and for involving the clergy in their social programs. Ironically, when Boumedienne came to power in June 1965, through a coup which toppled pro-Soviet Ahmed Ben Bella, the Soviets were apprehensive about his promise to restore the primacy of Algeria's Islamic heritage. According to Middle East specialists, he made it clear that Islam did not preclude "progressive" reforms. His policy, it is said, illustrated that Islam "promotes the growing popularity of the revolutionary democrats and favorably influences the peoples' attitudes."[37] Algeria has thus become a model which Soviet authorities clearly hope other Middle East friends will follow.

Throughout the 1980s, Islam continued to be a major research topic for the institutes and a significant concern for policymakers. Evgenii Primakov, summarizing the tasks facing orientalists, announced the creation of a working section on "Islam in Politics" which was to investigate the duality of Islamic political movements and the petty bourgeois nature of Islamic ideology. Moreover, Primakov proposed two related areas for study: (1) the influence and interrelationship between the religious factor and nationalism; and (2) class differentiation within the Islamic movement.[38] Some of the later interpretations cited above are clearly the results of these directions.

In the final analysis, Soviet experts have yet to come up with a totally satisfactory assessment of the Islamic revival. As noted above, they are clearly aware of its anti-Western potential. Simultaneously, they have not yet figured out either when it will turn against leftist forces or why it is such a widespread phenomenon. These investigations will likely continue well into the next decade because Islam will remain a potent force in the Middle East. Moreover, their ambiguous analyses notwithstanding, understanding the Islamic revolution forms a necessary backdrop for Soviet policy toward the Middle East and the Gulf War.

Notes

1. B. I. Ivanov and A. O. Tamazishvili, "Nauchnye issledovaniia instituta vostokovedeniia AN SSR v svete reshenii XXVI s'ezda KPSS," *Narody Azii i Afriki,* No. 2, 1982, p. 121.

2. For an interesting analysis of the interrelationships between the institutes and policymakers see Oded Eran, *The Mezhdunarodniki,* (Ramat Gan, Israel: Turtle Dove Press, 1979).

3. L. Shaidullina, "Goodwill Mission," *Nauka i religiia,* No. 3, 1981, pp. 23–24, abstracted in *Current Digest of the Soviet Press* (hereafter *CDSP*), Vol. XXXIII, No. 18, June 3, 1981, p. 13.

4. Based on discussions with Soviet officials and academics.

5. For a detailed analysis of the several constructs adopted by Soviet Third World experts see Carol R. Saivetz and Sylvia Woodby, *Soviet–Third World Relations* (Boulder, Colorado: Westview Press, 1985), Chapter 1.

6. V. Kudriavtsev, "Algeria on the Advance," *Izvestiia,* April 25, 1964, p. 1.

7. "V. Mayevskii on 'Conversations in Cairo,'" in "Soviet and UAR Views on Socialism," *Mizan,* No. 8, September, 1962, pp. 7–12.

8. V. Ovchinnikov, "Political Commentator's Notes," *Pravda,* February 13, 1979, p. 5 in *CDSP,* Vol. XXXI, No. 6, March 7, 1979, p. 15.

9. N. Prozhogin, "Stormy Time," *Pravda,* January 7, 1979, p. 4 in *CDSP,* Vol. XXXI, No. 1, January 31, 1979, p. 15.

10. May Day Slogans—1979, *CDSP,* Vol. XXXI, No. 7, March 14, 1979, p. 5.

11. A. M. Aliev, "Antimonarkhicheskaia i anti-imperialisticheskaia revoliutsiia v Irane," *Narody Azii i Afriki,* No. 3, 1979, p. 53.

12. L. Medvedko, "Islam and Liberation Revolutions," *New Times,* No. 43, 1979, p. 21.

13. See the discussion in R. A. Ul'ianovskii, "Iranskaia revoliutsiia i ee osobennosti," *Kommunist,* No. 10, 1982.

14. In October 1982, the Soviet Union initiated a new Persian radio series beamed at Iran. The editor/correspondent, V. Volinskii, was announced as a Persian specialist. This quotation is from a broadcast entitled "National Liberation Movements and Their Friends," October 31, 1983, in *JPRS,* 84861, December 2, 1983, p. 24.

15. Igor Sheftunov commentary: "What Is Hidden Behind the Curtain of the Invitation to Export the Islamic Revolution," *JPRS,* 84861, December 2, 1983, p. 22.

16. R.A. Ul'ianovskii, "International Life: Moral Principles in Politics and Policy in the Sphere of Morals; Iran—What Next?" *Literaturnaia Gazeta,* June 22, 1983, *Foreign Broadcast Information Service* (hereafter *FBIS*), *SOV* 83 127, June 30, 1983, p. H3. Italics added.

17. V. I. Maksimenko, "Analiz iranskoi revoliutsii 1978–1979 gg. v sovetskoi vostokovednoi literature," *Narody Azii i Afriki,* No. 3, 1987, p. 169, and S. L. Agaiev, "Levii radikalizm, revoliutsionnoi demokratizm i nauchnii sotsializm v stranakh vostoka," *Rabochii klass i sovremennii mir,* No. 3, 1984.

18. Maksimenko, "Analiz . . . ," p. 166.

19. Liudmila Polonskaia, "Major Trends in the Ideological Struggle," *Asia and Africa Today* (English), No. 3 (May–June), 1982, p. 2.

20. A. Ionova, "Islam and International Economic Cooperation," *Aziia i Afrika Segodnia,* No. 3, 1983, in *JPRS,* 84984, December 20, 1983, p. 17.

21. I. M. Smilianskaia, "Islam i problemy obshchestvennogo razvitiia arabskikh stran," *Narody Azii i Afriki,* No. 1, 1984, p. 109.

22. See "Vsesouznaia nauchnaia konferentsiia 'zakonomernosti i spetsifika razvitiia revoliutsionnogo protsessa v osvobodivshikhsia stranakh Afriki i Azii,'" *Narody Azii i Afriki,* No. 1, 1983, p. 128.

23. L. Polonskaia and A. Ionova, "Konseptsii 'islamskoiekonomiki': sotsial'naia sushchnost' i politicheskaia napravlennost'," *Mirovaia ekonomika i mezhdunarodnye otnosheniia,* No. 3, 1981, pp. 113, 116, 117.

24. *Pravda* and *Izvestiia,* February 24, 1981, in *CDSP,* Vol. XXXIII, No. 8, March 25, 1981, pp. 7, 8.

25. V. B. Kliashtorina, "<Vostok-Zapad> v kontekste sovremennoi iranskoi kul'turi," *Narody Azii i Afriki,* No. 3, 1985, pp. 47, 48.

26. Irina Zhmiuda, "Pakistan—Islamic Principles In The Country's Economy," *Asia and Africa Today* (English), No. 5, 1981, p. 40.

27. A. Germanovich and L. Medvedko, "A 'Revival of Islam' or Awakening of the People," *Nauka i religiia,* No. 7, July 1982, *JPRS,* 82288, November 22, 1982, p. 8.

28. E. Primakov, "Islam i protsessy obshchestvennogo razvitiia stran zarubezhnogo vostoka," *Voprosy Filosofii,* No. 8, 1980, pp. 61–62.

29. V. Zorin, "The World Today," August 5, 1982, *FBIS SOV* 82 152, August 6, 1982, p. H12.

30. Gabriel Hazak, "Afghanistan: The Nature of the Problem," *Rahva Haal,* August 27, 1983, p. 3 in *JPRS,* 84740, November 14, 1983, p. 2.

31. Salekh Muhammed Zeray, "Afghanistan: Following the Victorious Path of the April Revolution," *Partiinaia Zhizn',* No. 14, 1982, pp. 74–79, in *JPRS,* 81768, September 15, 1982, p. 20.

32. V. Volinskii, "Afghanistan's Popular Revolution and Its Opponents," in Farsi, November 12, 1983, *JPRS*, 84993, December 21, 1983, p. 6.

33. Germanovich and Medvedko, "A 'Revival of Islam' . . . ," p. 6.

34. *Ibid.*, p. 7.

35. "Tradition and Contemporaneity in the Social Development of Eastern Countries," *Asia and Africa Today* (English), No. 6, 1983, pp. 2, 21.

36. "Vsesouznaia. . . . ," p. 128.

37. Aleksandr Malshenko, "Algeria, Religious Tradition and the Policy of Revolutionary Democracy," *Asia and Africa Today*, No. 2, 1980, p. 38 and Germanovich and Medvedko, "A 'Revival of Islam'. . . ."

38. E. Primakov, "Aktualnye zadachi sovetskogo vostokovedeniia," *Narody Azii i Afriki*, No. 5, 1983.

2

The Iran-Iraq War

Origins of the Gulf War

The hostility between Gulf neighbors Iran and Iraq which culminated in war has its roots in the imperial past of the region. The dispute over the Shatt-al-Arab may be traced to the Persian–Ottoman tug-of-war which developed in the sixteenth century. Since then the territorial dispute has resulted in all-out wars and periods of short-lived peace. The border area—often times including Basra—was controlled by turns by the Persians and the Turks. In the nineteenth century, the British and Tsarist empires inserted their power into the area. The ensuing British–Russian "great game" necessitated controlling the rivalry between the two Mideast empires: Indeed, in 1843, Russia and Great Britain established a Turko–Persian commission to settle border questions.[1] The resulting treaty (the second treaty of Erzerum), which was more favorable to the Persians, temporarily demarcated the boundary; however, ethnic disputes continued to flare along the line.

Then, again in 1913, a new series of agreements established the international boundary at the low water mark of the Iranian shore line and further delineated the whole of the Turko–Persian border. This pre-World War I settlement was clearly more favorable to the Ottomans. Persia was required to relinquish certain territories along the Shatt and international access was permitted to the port of Khorramshahr. The Iranians, claiming that the collection of revenues by Iraq from ships on the Shatt violated the 1913 agreement, sought to reverse the situation.[2]

With the end of World War I and the collapse of the Ottoman Empire, Iraq emerged as an independent state—albeit under British control. Iran, seeking to gain concessions from Iraq, withheld recognition of the monarchy in Baghdad until 1929. When King Faisal I visited Teheran in 1932, the Iranians requested a border rectification on the Shatt. Following unsuccessful League of Nations participation, Iran and Iraq undertook bilateral negotiations. These resulted in a

1937 treaty which netted the Iranians a territorial gain opposite Abadan. Nonetheless, Baghdad continued to control most of the Shatt-al-Arab.

Between 1937 and 1975, there were several eruptions of the on-going border dispute. In 1968, with the accession to power of the Ba'ath Party, Iraq declared its intention to reassert control over the entire waterway. In response, in 1969, the Iranian government unilaterally abrogated the treaty. This abrogation coincided with a period of marked instability and radicalization in Iraq and opened an era of expansionism for Iran. In 1971, Teheran occupied three strategic islands in the Strait of Hormuz. Iraq, as the other contender for regional power, registered major international alarm and expelled 60,000 Iranians in retaliation.[3] Simultaneously, the Iranians provided military assistance to the Kurds of Iraq who were engaged in a long-term struggle against the central Baghdad government. Consequently, the years between 1969 and 1975 witnessed a propaganda war punctuated by border clashes.

Also in the early seventies, Soviet relations with each of the rivals grew. For Iraq, increasing isolation in the Arab world dictated closer ties with Moscow. In order to curry favor with the USSR, Baghdad went so far as to sign an agreement with the Communist Party of Iraq to create a national front. When then vice chairman, Saddam Hussein, travelled to the Soviet Union in February 1972 he called for a formal alliance with the USSR. The joint communique issued at the end of the visit stressed the increasing ties between the USSR and Iraq, and military and economic cooperation. Most importantly, the communique stated:

> Guided by a mutual desire for the further development and strengthening of the relations of friendship and comprehensive cooperation between the Soviet Union and the Republic of Iraq, the two sides have agreed, taking the present exchange of opinions into account, to study additional measures that could be undertaken in the near future adequately to strengthen the relations that have developed between the two states and to raise these relations to a new and higher level, *formulating them in a treaty.*[4]

And two months later a Friendship and Cooperation Treaty was signed in Baghdad by Soviet Premier Aleksei Kosygin and Iraqi President Hassan Al-Bakr. The treaty emphasized that the two signatories would consult each other in the event of a crisis and that neither would engage in alliances designed to threaten the other. Article nine, moreover, stated that both the USSR and Iraq will "continue to develop cooperation in strengthening their defense capabilities." (See appendix for full text.) This was only the third such treaty after Egypt and India, and the first in the Gulf zone.

During the same period, Soviet ties with Iran entered a period which Alvin Z. Rubinstein has called economic detente.[5] In the mid-sixties, the Soviets offered a $300 million credit and signed agreements to build a steel mill at Isfahan and a gas pipeline. Soviet–Iranian economic relations flowered in the wake of these agreements. As with the early steel mills in India and the Aswan Dam in Egypt, the pipeline deal was implemented only after the US had refused to help the Iranians construct it. For their part, the Soviets derived direct economic benefits from the deal in that they could use the Iranian gas domestically, while selling their native supplies to the East European countries. After the completion of the pipeline in 1970, Iran became the USSR's primary supplier of natural gas. In the fall of 1972, during an official visit of the Shah and his wife to Moscow, the two countries signed a fifteen-year economic treaty. The provisions of the agreement included several industrial projects and contained the pronounced intention to increase economic cooperation.

Yet, despite the great fanfare with which the economic agreement was announced, Gulf politics intruded into the negotiations. The communique which announced the economic treaty also referred to "frank" discussions, no doubt reflecting disagreements over the Iraqi–Soviet friendship treaty. In light of the long-standing border dispute between Iran and Iraq, the treaty, which promised to strengthen Iraqi defensive capabilities, must have alarmed the Iranians. Then in 1974, a major natural gas pricing dispute erupted which jolted the bilateral ties. As the international price of oil and natural gas rose, the Iranians attempted to force the USSR to pay the going rate. However, the Soviets not only refused to agree to Iranian demands, but also claimed that the Iranian price increases were instigated by Western imperialists. Ultimately, Moscow agreed in August to a compromise price that was below the world rate, but higher than the price the Kremlin paid previously.

Almost simultaneously with the resolution of the price dispute, relations between Iran and Iraq deteriorated again. Moscow repeatedly called for a peaceful resolution to the conflict. At the Kremlin dinner honoring the Shah in 1974, then Soviet President Nikolai Podgorny stated:

> Proceeding from this premise, we want to say in all candor that the existing tension in relations between Iran and Iraq does not correspond to the interests of the cause of peace; we have advocated and continue to advocate the settlement of Iranian–Iraqi differences by these countries themselves at the negotiating table.

Yet, in his response the Shah noted that if Iraq "did not adhere so zealously to the legacy of British imperialism, there would be no problems between us."[6]

This 1974 flare-up of the Iran–Iraq dispute was ended through Algerian mediation at an OPEC meeting in Algiers in March 1975. The 1975 accord included the following terms.

1. Iran would stop aid to the Kurdish rebellion in Iraq.
2. The *thalweg* principle—the center of the major navigable channel—would determine the border along the whole Shatt-al-Arab.
3. Iraq would drop its opposition to the Iranian occupation of the three Gulf islands.
4. Baghdad promised compensation to the 60,000 Shi'is previously expelled from Iraq.

The Soviets for whom the dispute was a major foreign policy complication were pleased by the Algiers accord. With a temporary halt to the hostilities, Iraqi–Soviet relations remained stable and Iranian–Soviet relations improved. By the same token, the political rivalry between Baghdad and Teheran continued unabated. Each provided aid to the opposing side in the war between Dhofari rebels and the sultan of Oman and each made different proposals for collective security arrangements in the region. In the view of Nadav Safran, in the period between 1975–1979 there was a triangular balance among Saudi Arabia, Iran, and Iraq in their bids for Gulf leadership.[7] The situation was to change dramatically by the late seventies. The overthrow of the monarchy in Iran and the establishment of the Islamic regime there had a profound impact on regional dynamics and Iraqi foreign policy calculations.

The Khomeini revolution in Iran represented an old and new force in the region. Islamic revivalism by itself was not new, but its embodiment in a powerful government was a phenomenon with which the Muslim world had to contend. Khomeini's brand of revolution included calls to all Shi'is in the region to rise up against their Sunni masters. Saddam Hussein, as the Sunni leader of a predominantly Shi'i country, had particular reasons to feel threatened. Moreover, he is the head of a regime and party which espouses a secular socialist ideology. Indeed, the Iranian revolution exacerbated pre-existing ideological tensions between "progressive" Iraq and monarchical, now fundamentalist, Iran. Finally, Saddam Hussein had, a year earlier, expelled the Ayatollah Ruhollah Khomeini from Iraq where he had lived for sixteen years.

Another cause of the Gulf War was the age-old dispute over the Shatt-al-Arab. It should be remembered that Iraq had made territorial concessions to Iran in 1975 in return for peace and an end to Teheran's support of the Kurdish rebellion. By 1980, Iraq felt that its security was again threatened by Teheran. The conflict over navigational rights was, therefore, a logical issue for the Iraqis to seize. This is not to diminish the importance of the Shatt to Baghdad. Iraq is, after all, the only OPEC member whose livelihood is dependent upon the goodwill of its neighbors. A glance at the map will reveal that the Shatt-al-Arab is vital as it provides access to Iraq's major port at Basra, some forty-seven miles up-river.

On October 31, 1979, the Iraqi ambassador in Beirut outlined the Baghdad government's demands on the new leadership in Teheran. He called for a revision of the 1975 Algiers accord; Iranian withdrawal from the three Gulf islands; and self-rule for the Arabs of Khuzistan. This last can be seen as Iraqi retaliation for the appeals to Shi'is within Iraq. Between October 1979 and September 22, 1980, Baghdad pursued a carefully orchestrated plan of securing support for its actions and establishing a leadership position for itself in the Gulf. In a bid for regional power status, Saddam Hussein announced, on February 8, 1980, a Charter for Pan-Arab Action. The proposed charter called for nonalignment and cooperation and was well received by several Gulf states. In August, Hussein travelled to Saudi Arabia to garner Saudi backing for the upcoming war effort. Although the Iraqi president claimed to have secured Saudi support, the government in Riyadh initially kept a low profile. On September 9, the Iraqis advanced to regain the territory they ceded in 1975. Then on September 17, Baghdad abrogated the 1975 Algiers accord. And finally, on September 22, Iraq launched an all-out invasion of Iran.

Early Soviet Policy Toward the Gulf War

At the outbreak of the war, Soviet observers claimed that the conflict was a purely regional one from which neither side could benefit. They also charged that the US hoped to use the war for its own ends. *Komsomolskaia Pravda* alleged that the CIA was fanning the flames of war and *Izvestiia*'s commentator wrote that the war provided a pretext for the United States to promote an association of pro-American states.[8] An *International Affairs* (Moscow) article spelled out the supposed alliance in more detail: "[g]uided by its expansionist plans, the US is striving to fashion a military–political alliance in the Middle East which would rest upon the money and oil of Saudi Arabia, the human resources of Egypt and the military potential of Israel."[9]

The war alarmed the Soviet Union because the hostilities had evoked a major US response. Prior to the outbreak of the war, the USSR's regional position appeared very strong. In fact, as the situation in Iran in 1979–1980 remained highly unstable, many Western analysts expected a Soviet move into Iran. They were divided, however, as to whether Moscow would seek to absorb northern areas such as Azerbaijan or continue further south to seize Iranian oil fields. With hindsight, it seems that the most propitious time for Soviet armed intervention would have been between February 1979, Khomeini's return to Teheran, and December 1979, the Soviet invasion of Afghanistan. This was a period in which the Khomeini forces had not yet consolidated their hold on power and disarray and uncertainty pervaded Washington. (Unclear as to what Khomeini's accession to power would portend and divided over what kinds of policies to pursue, the Carter administration seemed unlikely, at this time, to respond militarily to any Soviet action.) At the same time, the USSR would have had to carefully weigh a decision to intervene. Moscow lacked a pretext or "host" to invite in the Soviet troops. The Kremlin leadership would have needed to consider the response of the Iranian population to any invasion of their territory. Moreover, the USSR would also need to assess the response of the other regional actors to their policy. Finally, the invasion routes themselves presented major obstacles: The treacherous mountain terrain has few roads, limited rail service, and many potential points of interdiction.

Although the political and military consequences of an invasion might have been great, there is evidence of Soviet military maneuvers in the southern zone in the summer of 1980. Intelligence reports indicate that Soviet troops, in what the USSR calls the southern theater, were put on a higher degree of readiness than normal. However, by mid-September they had stood down.

All analyses of the regional power balance give the decided edge to the Soviets because of their proximity to the Gulf. The geographic advantage will not disappear, but the US and its NATO allies moved in the initial weeks and months of the Gulf War to undercut the USSR's advantage. At the least, they sought to signal their concern over regional politics. Within a week following the Iraqi attack, Airborne Warning and Control Aircraft (AWACs) were dispatched to Saudi Arabia and on October 5 the US sent additional radar equipment to Riyadh. Thus, by the second week in October, intelligence operations were in place. Then on October 11, Washington announced that a guided missile cruiser had been sent to the Gulf along with two tanker planes destined for the Saudis. Almost simultaneously, sixty British, US, French, and Australian warships were assembled in the Indian Ocean. Several of the NATO countries intensified their contact with the Gulf states, while the US did the same with Oman and Saudi Arabia.

Alarmed at US efforts and clearly hoping to limit the infusion of the American presence in the region, Leonid Brezhnev proposed that the Gulf region be demilitarized. In a speech delivered while on an official visit to India in December 1980, the Soviet leader advanced the following plan:

- not to establish foreign military bases in the area of the Persian Gulf and adjacent islands; not to deploy nuclear or any other weapons
- not to use and not to threaten the use of force against the countries of the Persian Gulf area; not to interfere in their internal affairs
- to respect the status of nonalignment, chosen by Persian Gulf states; not to draw them into miliary groupings with the participation of nuclear powers
- to respect the sovereign right of the states of the region to their natural resources
- not to raise any obstacles or threats to normal trade exchange and the use of sea lanes that link the states of that region with other countries of the world[10]

This proposal, particularly the first and third items, was obviously designed to forestall the acceptability to the regional actors of a US presence.

If the Soviets hoped to cope easily with the war by stirring up anti-American sentiments, their actual dealings with the two combatants proved far more complex. On September 22, 1980, Iraqi foreign minister Tariq Aziz flew to Moscow. The Iraqis claimed that he went only to brief Soviet officials;[11] however, it would seem more likely that the foreign minister went to request additional arms assistance. The Kremlin was not terribly forthcoming: Some Soviet-made spare parts did arrive in Baghdad, although they were probably already in the arms pipeline. No new major arms deals resulted from the trip; in fact, the USSR, still the major Iraqi supplier, held up military shipments to Baghdad during the first winter of the war. Yet, in an effort to keep the Saddam Hussein regime on the line, Moscow simultaneously permitted its Warsaw Pact allies to increase significantly their military sales to Iraq. That first winter Iraq received 100 T-55 tanks from Poland, Bulgaria, and East Germany.[12] Moreover, Moscow apparently permitted Iraq to use high altitude TU 22 bombers which were in Baghdad's arsenal, but which were under tight Soviet restrictions.[13] Further reports surfaced about the kinds of arms assistance received by Iraq. According to an April 1981 TASS dispatch, Baghdad accepted delivery of arms from Somalia, North Yemen, and Egypt, all transshipped through Saudi ports.[14] William Quandt, in his book on Saudi Arabia, acknowledges the Saudi role in equipping Iraq, but claims that Soviet material as well was off-loaded at Saudi ports. He writes: ". . . [e]arly in 1981 the Saudis allowed Iraq to take delivery of 100 East European tanks at Saudi Red Sea ports. This soon became regular practice with East European and Soviet ships calling at the small port of Qadima north of Jidda to unload shipments of arms for Iraq."[15]

On the Iranian side of the ledger, military assistance began to flow from Libya and Syria. By the second week of October 1980, Libya had begun an airlift of supplies to Teheran. Syria, because of its long-standing rivalry with Iraq, also transshipped equipment to Iran. In both cases, the deliveries were of Soviet equipment and it is presumed that the Kremlin approved the transfers.

Within two weeks of the outbreak of the war, the USSR and Syria signed a Friendship and Cooperation Treaty. Although President Assad pressed for the treaty because of Syrian domestic political considerations, Soviet President Leonid Brezhnev seemingly used the occasion of the signing of the treaty to underscore tacit Soviet support for the Syrian arms supply to Iran. In his speech at the Kremlin dinner honoring Assad and the friendship treaty, Brezhnev dwelled at length on the then two-week-old war. He claimed that the imperialists wanted to use the war to divide Arab ranks. "The Soviet Union has given and will continue to give a strong rebuff to such a policy. And we are glad that in this respect we hold a common stand with Syria and other peace-loving states."[16]

While all observers agree that during the initial stages of the war, Moscow's professed neutrality tilted toward Teheran, a few see evidence of more direct Soviet support. Shahram Chubin, for example, writing in *Foreign Affairs,* alleged that Soviet backing of Teheran consisted of warning of the impending attack, easing Iranian concerns regarding the USSR's intentions so as to permit reassignment of Iranian troops, and providing satellite information.[17]

The Soviet policy might have worked in the short term, but the war quickly bogged down. If, as suggested above, Saddam Hussein had counted on the weakness of the Iranian military due to political instability, then within two months he was proven wrong. First, the Iraqis did not succeed in knocking out the Iranian air force. Second, they advanced as far as the port area of Khorramshahr, but did not take the city. In addition, the Iraqi forces encountered stiff resistance around Abadan. Finally, the Iranians successfully blockaded Iraqi ports, leaving Baghdad to seek alternative routes for its oil exports and arms imports.[18] By November, military positions were frozen and, in these conditions of stalemate, each side had to search repeatedly for military supplies. The Iraqis sent Tariq Aziz back to Moscow to seek an uninterrupted arms supply. Other Iraqi officials travelled to Eastern Europe and to Britain and France.

The war remained stalemated until March 1981 when Iran launched some local counter offensives. Indeed, throughout 1981, the series of Iranian counter attacks continued. In September, the Iranians success-fully lifted the siege of Abadan and then in November positions refroze. Throughout this period, Soviet propaganda themes remained constant. In both Arabic and Farsi broadcasts to the region, Moscow emphasized the benefits of the war to Israel and imperialism and urged each of the combatants to end the war. For the USSR, the questions became how long the balancing act could be maintained and what were its consequences for Soviet bilateral relations with the combatants.

From the Soviet perspective, as long as the US diplomatic personnel were held in Teheran, not only did the US look impotent, but the possibility of US military assistance to Iran also seemed nonexistent. The end of the Iranian hostage crisis, through Algerian mediation, removed a potential obstacle to an Iranian-American rapprochement. The Kremlin could take no comfort in Iranian behavior. In February 1981, Prime Minister Raja'i, in a meeting with the Soviet ambassador, criticized the continuing occupation of Afghanistan and chided the USSR for not condemning the initial Iraqi attack. And, in addition to the Iranian rhetoric which labelled the USSR "the lesser Satan," press reports in Teheran began to evidence a distinct anti-Soviet flavor. The Soviets responded in broadcasts to Iran that they possessed only a friendly attitude toward Teheran and that the Iranian press miscon-strued Soviet policy.

Moscow fared little better on the Iraqi front. Adding to the already complex relationship between the USSR and Iraq, the Iraqi Communist Party delegate to the twenty-sixth congress of the CPSU took the occasion of his speech to denounce the Saddam Hussein regime.[19] Aziz Muhammad's attack on the Ba'ath leadership was coupled with a call for Iraqi withdrawal from Iran. The speech may be seen as both a measure of the attenuation of Soviet–Iraqi ties and, from the viewpoint of Baghdad, just another indication of Moscow's tilt toward Teheran.

By April, the Soviets appeared to be seeking actively an amelioration of their connections to Baghdad. On the occasion of the ninth anni-versary of the friendship treaty with Iraq, Moscow radio reported the celebrations at Friendship House in Moscow, but did not mention the Iran–Iraq War. Additionally, the telegram sent by the Soviet leadership to Saddam Hussein claimed that:

The Soviet Union is prepared to continue developing relations with Iraq on the basis of mutual interest in strengthening friendship and cooperation between our countries and for the benefit of the Soviet and Iraqi peoples and for the sake of the cause of peace and international security.[20]

Finally, at about the same time, the chairman of the State Committee for Foreign Economic Relations, Semen Skachkov, was dispatched to Baghdad where he met with Saddam Hussein. Their meeting was designed, according to the reports, to implement previously signed economic accords.

Nonetheless, Iraq indicated by April 1981 a willingness to reevaluate ties with the US. In a *Washington Post* interview published April 19, 1981, Tariq Aziz said that Iraq favored a dialogue with Washington, although at that point the resumption of diplomatic relations was not foreseen.[21] Aziz's statement was in response to clear signals from the Reagan administration that Washington's attitude toward Iraq was changing. That April, the sale of five Boeing aircraft was approved and Deputy Assistant Secretary of State Morris Draper travelled to Baghdad.

In June 1981, the Israelis bombed a French-built nuclear reactor at Osirak, Iraq. The Kremlin used the incident to attack US imperialism and more importantly to try yet again to rebuild its ties to the Saddam Hussein regime. Within weeks of the bombing, Iraqi first deputy prime minister Taha Yasin Ramadan went to Moscow. The conversations in the USSR capital which ostensibly dealt with expanding cooperation in several spheres were said to have taken place in a "friendly" atmosphere. Washington, for its part, evidenced further reevaluations of the relationship with Baghdad. The US voted in the Security Council to condemn the Israeli raid on the nuclear reactor.

It should be noted that this occurred at the same time as Bani Sadr was relieved as President of Iran. The possibility of a mediated settlement of the war disappeared with his removal. But the victory of the clerical forces which his ouster signalled militated against a rapprochement between the US and Iran. Although the Soviets may have welcomed the diminished chances of better relations between Washington and Teheran, they also needed to contend with the fact that many of the victorious clerical factions were intensely anti-Soviet.

As the war continued into 1982, the political leanings of the clergy in Teheran became increasingly important and distressful to the Kremlin. Soviet media coverage of the domestic turmoil in Iran suggests that Moscow was trying to salvage what it could from a deteriorating situation. In early 1982, the press stressed the USSR's support for antimonarchical forces during the revolution and lavished praise on the growth of Soviet–Iranian economic relations. Yet, as early as March, reporters noted problems in Soviet–Iranian relations including the nonaccreditation of Soviet correspondents, disbandment of Soviet–Iranian cultural groups, and the closure of the Soviet consulate in Resht. Moreover, *Pravda* correspondent Pavel Demchenko, a veteran Middle East observer, wrote:

> We know that the Shi'ite clergymen who hold the reins of government in Iran are not uniform in their political beliefs or social positions. There are various conservative factions . . . with extreme right-wing views. It seems that it is these groups who want to put up obstacles to the expansion of Soviet–Iranian relations even though such action could harm the Iranian economy and Iran's ability to fight imperialist pressure.[22]

Ironically, it was during this spring that the USSR was presumed to have achieved its greatest influence over Iranian affairs. Reports circulated in the West that the pro-Soviet Tudeh Party was gaining increasingly influential roles in key Iranian ministries. At the same time, the Baghdad–Washington flirtation continued. The Reagan administration removed Iraq from the list of nations said to support terrorism, thus clearing the way for Iraq to receive several export licenses. At the time, several Western analysts feared that if the US were to reestablish diplomatic relations with Iraq, then Iran would fall totally under Soviet influence.

Also in March 1982, a new stage in the war began when Iran sent 200,000 troops into Iraq in the North. Several weeks later, Syria severed the flow of Iraqi hard currency by closing the Iraqi pipeline. That May, the Iranians expelled Iraqi troops from Khorramshahr. In June, endangered Iraq declared a unilateral cease-fire and withdrawal from Iranian territory. Baghdad also announced its readiness to negotiate without conditions. Teheran ignored Iraq's signals and Iranian troops crossed into Iraq in July. In the new prevailing circumstances, the Kremlin faced new risks: Could the Kremlin afford an Iraqi defeat? How would other Soviet allies react to the defeat of a Soviet treaty partner? Given the USSR's concern over the tenor of Iranian politics, could the Kremlin leadership live wih a victorious Iran? A careful analysis of Soviet statements and behavior reveals Moscow's impatience and alarm about the continuation of the war.

First, journalists such as Yuri Glukhov, longtime *Pravda* correspondent, charged that the imperialists sought to prolong the war. And Igor Beliaev, an economist and curently chief of *Literaturnaia Gazeta*'s foreign policy department, alleged that the war served as justification for joint American–Arab military maneuvers. Additionally, he claimed that the same Arab states in the past had expressed concern about the

US presence in the region.[23] These Soviet responses were elicited by a series of US actions and statements. The Reagan administration undertook to shore up Baghdad's position by providing nearly $1 billion worth of commodity credits. Washington also voted for a Security Council resolution which condemned Iran and supported an arms embargo against Teheran. Moreover, as Iranian troops crossed into Iraq, the US reportedly offered to hold joint military maneuvers with moderate Persian Gulf states.[24]

Second, on the anniversary of the Soviet–Iraqi Friendship and Cooperation Treaty, the Soviets heaped praise upon Iraq and upon the state of relations between Moscow and Baghdad. Soviet aid was said to have furthered Iraqi prosperity and the treaty itself "strengthened the unity and cohesiveness of all anti-imperialist forces in the Arab world." Yet the Soviets, ever concerned with their deteriorating relations with the Iranians and their patron–client relationship with Syria, added that the Iraqi treaty was directed against no one else.[25] And, on the occasion of Iraqi independence day (July), the Soviet Union again went to great lengths to reinvigorate Soviet–Iraqi relations. According to Soviet international affairs experts, since the Ba'ath came to power in 1968, Iraq consolidated its economic independence, developed its national economy, and implemented transformations in agriculture. All of these policies constitute part of the prescribed development course recommended for "progressive" Third World states.

Third, early in June 1982, Tariq Aziz made a quick trip to Moscow to meet with Soviet officials. In all probability, the visit had as much to do with the mounting tensions in Lebanon—the Israeli invasion occurred two days later—as with the Iran–Iraq War. Nevertheless, two weeks later the Iraqis announced the pullout from Iran. The troop withdrawal received high marks from the Soviets.

The Lebanese situation, by itself, had profound repercussions for the whole Middle East. The impact of the Gulf War on Soviet sponsorship of the Arab cause will be discussed in Chapter 4. In the context of the Soviet–American regional balance, Lebanon played a significant role. To the Soviets, it must have appeared that America was on the march in the Middle East. Not only had the US beefed up its presence in the Gulf, but it also—as a result of the Israeli invasion and occupation—had taken on a major role in ensuring the PLO evacuation from Beirut and in stationing US marines there.

Fourth, also in June, both Teheran and Baghdad received new Soviet ambassadors. It may be assumed that Moscow hoped to renew the flow of ties with both countries by bringing in new knowlegeable faces. The new ambassador to Iran, V. Boldyrev, was a career foreign service officer who served as deputy head of the section on Middle East countries. Iraq's new ambassador, Viktor Minin, worked in the central apparatus of the Ministry of Foreign Affairs and was chief of the Middle East department.

Fifth, V. Volinskii, a Persian specialilst whose radio talks were designed to dispel "misconceptions" about the Soviet Union, said in an obvious stab at the Shi'i clergy and at Khomeini's pronounced goal of unseating the Hussein regime: "Our stand on the Iran–Iraq War was clear from the very beginning and still is. We oppose the intervention by any other country in the domestic affairs of another. No one but the people of the country concerned has the right to say that the regime in another is to his liking or not."[26]

Sixth, Soviet impatience with the conduct of the war and with Iranian anti-Soviet propaganda may well have been magnified by President Saddam Hussein's comments in November 1982. The Iraqi president is quoted as saying that Iraq's friendship treaty with the Soviet Union "ha[d] not worked." At a news conference with American correspondents, he indicated Iraqi satisfaction with the treaty until the outbreak of the Iran–Iraq War. Saddam Hussein added that Iraq was engaged in a "dialogue" with Moscow to better relations, while at the same time, Baghdad was moving to improve relations with the US.[27]

Finally, Iranian anti-Sovietism coupled with Soviet fears of an Iranian victory in the war led to a reinstatement of the arms connection between Moscow and Baghdad. According to most observers, arms deliveries were resumed by September–October 1982: Iraq received MiG 25s, T 72 tanks, and SA 8 missiles.[28] Reports of an increase in the number of Soviet advisors in Iraq also reached the West. According to one estimate, there were 1500 advisors in place in October 1982.[29]

Publically, of course, USSR spokesmen continued to profess neutrality. Even as the arms trade to Baghdad was renewed, Moscow denied providing equipment to either combatant. In an interview with the Kuwaiti *al Watan* G. Trofimenko stated that the Soviet Union was not interested in prolonging the war. He added: "We are very cautious regarding this war and we do not want to offer military aid to this or that party because this will deepen the dispute between the two countries and will prolong the war."[30]

Continuing Hostilities

At year's end, the dilemma for the Soviets was unresolved. Iran proved unpliable and Iraq further distanced itself from the Kremlin. Although the arms pipeline to Baghdad reopened, Syria, Libya, and North Korea supplied Soviet weaponry to Teheran. Moscow's propagandists continued to lament the status of Soviet–Iranian relations. The last of Volinskii's Farsi language broadcasts urged better relations on Teheran, but complained that while Moscow sought the amelioration of ties "it took two hands to clap."[31] By the same token, Iraqi–Soviet relations remained attenuated. In a long article on the Gulf War, the Soviet weekly *New Times* stressed not only the wastefulness and sense-lessness of the war, but also the common anti-imperialism of the two combatants. While underscoring the Muslim heritage of the two (the Sunni-Shi'a difference was not mentioned), and while calling for a speedy, peaceful resolution to the conflict, *New Times* seemed to take a slightly pro-Iraqi stand. The author implicitly criticized the Teheran regime for rejecting a cease-fire and UN mediation efforts.[32] Ultimately, the USSR still felt the need to justify its intense interest in the war, if not its involvement. As Dmitri Volskii wrote:

> For the Soviet Union is not seeking "profit at the expense of the Muslim people's interests."
> The battle area is within a stone's throw of the Soviet Union's southern borders. Who wants a blazing fire or even smoldering coals on his doorstep?[33]

A month after Leonid Brezhnev's death in November, Ramadan and Aziz travelled to Moscow for what was billed as a two-day working meeting. According to reports, the two Iraqi officials returned home optimistic about Soviet positions. These same sources reported that the new Soviet leadership had shifted to a pro-Iraqi stance.[34] Yet, despite the problems the USSR experienced with the clerical regime in Teheran, Yuri Andropov's regime recognized the centrality of Iran. One of the first Farsi broadcasts beamed to Iran after the Andropov succession stressed the new party leader's commitment to foreign policies begun under Brezhnev. The program stressed Moscow's alleged role in the Iranian struggle against despotism;[35] but later broadcasts claimed that the full potential of Soviet–Iranian relations had not been realized.

The Iranian offensives of 1982 continued into 1983 with the Iraqis repelling several Iranian thrusts. The persisting Iranian pressure on Iraq alarmed the Soviets, coming as it did at a time of marked deterioration in Soviet–Iranian relations. In February, the Khomeini regime cracked down on the Tudeh party and arrested its leadership, including Nurredin Kianuri, the party's secretary. Following the collapse of the monarchy, Kianuri returned to Teheran from exile in Eastern Europe. He had succeeded Iarj Iskandari, who, although long-time leader of the party, was opposed to cooperating with Khomeini. In the years between 1979 and 1983, the Tudeh tread a careful path which balanced its pro-Soviet positions with support for the clerical regime. The party managed to survive the upheavals in Iranian political life, despite its support for the Soviet invasion of Afghanistan and its neutral stand on the Iran–Iraq War.

It should be noted in this context that the Soviet attitude toward local communist parties has always been ambivalent. On the one hand, as leader of the socialist bloc, Moscow had to recognize these sometimes small local groups, which indeed provided the USSR wih an additional policy option under certain circumstances. On the other hand, where cordial state-to-state relations existed and where practical considerations dictated, the Soviets showed themselves to be more than willing to sacrifice local communist interests. Obversely, Third World clients often used their policies toward these homegrown communists as signals to Moscow. In some cases communists were permitted to participate in coalition governments both to propitiate the Kremlin and to indicate pleasure with Soviet foreign policy. But in other instances, crackdowns on communist activity sent a ready sign to Moscow that its policies were not acceptable or that its meddling in local affairs had to stop.

The arrest of the Tudeh leadership—including an April recantation by Kianuri on Iranian television—probably resulted from domestic as well as foreign policy considerations. The Tudeh was the last independent group permitted to function and its decimation stemmed from Khomeini's drive to finalize the consolidation of power. Even the USSR took note of this process of weeding out the opposition. Simultaneously, the crackdown may be seen as retaliation for the renewal of military assistance to Iraq. The Soviet Union issued a vehement denunciation of the espionage charges and the arrests. *Pravda* charged "reactionary conservative circles" with striking a blow against internal patriotic forces and Soviet–Iranian relations at a time when the new political order in Iran faced counterrevolutionary attacks. The editorial concluded by reminding readers that the Soviet Union expected only friendship and reciprocity.[36] Soviet–Iranian relations deteriorated still further in May when Teheran expelled eighteen Soviet diplomats. Protesting the expulsion, *Pravda* accused "some representatives" of the Iranian authorities of exploiting the revolution and trying to upset Soviet–Iranian relations.[37] Soviet broadcasts to Iran stressed that anti-Soviet statements benefited only the United States.[38]

During the summer, Iraq threatened to destroy Iranian oil facilities and in fact struck at Kharg Island. Iran, in turn, threatened to close the straits of Hormuz. Alarmed over the escalation of the war, Moscow issued more strident denunciations of Iranian intransigence and increased its arms assistance to Iraq. The tilt toward Iraq that became visible a year earlier was readily apparent in official statements and press reports. In mid-June, then-foreign minister Andrei Gromyko said in a speech before the Supreme Soviet: "We have friendly relations with Iraq. We are *for* normal relations of friendship with Iran as well." Responding specifically to the expulsion of the Soviet diplomats from Iran, Gromyko continued: "In short the USSR will act with regard to whether Iran wishes to reciprocate its actions and maintain normal relations with us or whether it has different intentions"[39] This policy of reciprocity remained in effect until the summer of 1985. Aleksandr Bovin, one of the most prominent Soviet foreign policy commentators, noted in October that although Iraq had actually launched the war, Iran "helped to create the conflict" by inciting Iraq's Shi'is to overthrow the Ba'ath regime. In the article, Bovin also mentioned Iran's use of "fanatical youths" to pursue the war effort.[40]

Despite the pronounced sympathy for the Iraqi position and despite the reopening of the arms pipeline, the Soviets did not reap the expected gains from their tilt toward Baghdad. Politically, despite Moscow's wooing of Baghdad, the latter seemed intent on thawing relations with the US. The Iraqis, it appeared, would not soon forget the implicit support for Iran at the start of the war. In August 1982, Representative Stephen Solarz visited Saddam Hussein. During their conversations— which were not published until January 1983—Hussein made several conciliatory gestures. Moscow, for its part, appeared to be trying to buy Baghdad back from the West and from the growing centrist Arab camp. Yet, while appreciative of Soviet support, Iraq also made significant arms purchases in the West. Faced with a continuing Iranian assault, Iraq threatened to use French-built Exocet missiles against Iranian oil facilities. Baghdad already possessed the missiles, but in 1983, applied to France to supply super Etendard fighters. When Tariq Aziz travelled to Paris in May 1983 he again indicated Baghdad's desire to buy the planes. The deal was clinched and the delivery of the planes was reported in the fall.

The persistent tensions in the Baghdad–Moscow alliance were apparent when Tariq Aziz flew to Moscow in November 1983. Official Soviet statements described the talks as "frank," a term which usually denotes disagreements. Soviet concern over the consequences of the French deliveries was manifested in anti-American invective. Not only did the Kremlin appear to fear an enlargement in the scale of the conflict, but it also saw the potential widening of the war as an additional pretext for US military activity. *Izvestiia* reported debates in Washington regarding US abandonment of its neutrality in the same breath as it condemned plans for military operations to protect Western oil supplies.[41]

In all, Moscow's pro-Iranian stance backfired; the intentions of a fundamentalist Iran must have frightened policymakers; and Iraq's increased reliance on Western technology lessened Soviet leverage. 1984 seemed to bring Moscow's worst fears to reality. In the first place, the Reagan administration reaffirmed its stake in the Gulf. At the beginning of the year, Washington warned all planes and ships not to come within five miles of US planes or naval forces or risk drawing fire. Then in February, the US reiterated its commitment to keep open the Strait of Hormuz as the land war between Iraq and Iran heated up again. Iraq successfully parried Iranian attacks except around the Majnun oil fields. In retaliation for the Iranian advances, Iraq used its Exocet missiles for the first time on March 27 to attack shipping bound for Kharg Island. In April, the Shatt-al-Arab became the scene of heavy fighting. The intensification of the war prompted harsh statements from two authoritative Soviet spokesmen. Evgenii Primakov, currently director of the Institute of World Economics and International Affairs, stated in an *International Affairs* article that the US was preparing for a "tough confrontation" with the Soviet Union on global and regional levels simultaneously.[42] Equally strident in his condemnation of the continuation of the Gulf War and of US policy was Karen Brutents, deputy director of the International Department of the CPSU. In a "Studio 9" television roundtable he said:

> I would add to the fact that this is a senseless war, it is also a dangerous and harmful one. Dangerous, because it is being played out at a very sensitive . . . point. Petroleum routes of world significance pass through here, and the imperialist powers, particularly the United States, are already using this to justify their military presence in this zone, in the Persian Gulf region, and now even for planned military intervention.
>
> Further, this war has somehow cut Iran and Iraq—and these are very important states in the region—from the development of events in this region, from opposition to US–Zionist plans. They have seized one another in such a grip that they are unable to grasp other events or affairs.[43]

Other press commentaries echoed these themes. In some, the West was accused of seeking direct control over the region and in others the two combatants were portrayed as being at the mercy of petrodollar economics and Western arms merchants.

Concomitantly, Soviet relations with Iran deteriorated still further and those with Iraq seemed to remain stable, but cool. In February 1984, the Khomeini regime, capping a year-long clampdown on the Tudeh and chill in relations with Moscow, executed several of the communist activists arrested earlier. The Kremlin complained of anti-communist hysteria coupled with an anti-Soviet campaign. Yet, ever mindful of keeping the door to Iran ajar, *Pravda* issued only a Tudeh statement which called those executed true patriots.[44] The Iraqis, at the same time, annoyed Moscow by continuing to move closer to the US. Indeed, by November 1984, the Iraqi government would reestablish diplomatic ties with Washington after seventeen years.

In February/March, however, the amelioration process was disrupted by charges that Baghdad had used chemical weapons to repulse the Iranian offensive. Moscow jumped at the opportunity provided by the lull to sign a new economic cooperation agreement in March and to host Iraq's deputy prime minister Ramadan in April. *Pravda* described the talks as "friendly," but in its coverage, seemed to downplay the Iran–Iraq War.[45] Ironically the chemical weapons issue would not work completely to the USSR's advantage. The Soviets themselves did not escape from the political fallout: Reports circulated that charged Soviet technicians with training the Iraqis in the use of chemical weapons. These press reports were widespread enough that Moscow felt the need to rebut the charges. *Krasnaia zvezda,* among others, accused Iran and the imperialist West with an orchestrated slander campaign.[46]

The continuing touchy relations with each of the combatants was to take a back seat to the widening of the war in the spring. Saddam Hussein reiterated his determination to blockade Kharg Island, while the Iranian air force continued its activities in the Gulf. Saudi Arabia declared an exclusion zone up to sixty miles off the coast and Washington supplied Riyadh with 400 stingers and 200 launchers to bolster Saudi defenses. By May, Soviet observers were issuing increasingly shrill denunciations of US policy. Soviet UN representative Oleg Troyanovskii attacked the sale of the stingers. *Pravda* and *Izvestiia* as well as both Farsi and Arabic broadcasts all referred to the "massing" of US military force, and some analysts alleged that Israel was preparing for direct military intervention in the Gulf. The tanker war escalated in May with Iranian attacks on Saudi and Kuwaiti tankers. Then on June 4, Saudi Arabia, with the assistance of US AWACs, shot down an Iranian fighter. The initial TASS dispatch noted the incident, but centered on US involvement. The report noted that Iran and Iraq each condemned the US involvement as well.[47]

In light of the escalation of the conflict, especially Saudi participation, the stream of anti-American invective acquired a sense of urgency. The Soviets feared that a permanent US presence might be accepted by the regional powers. This concern may be seen in the Primakov article previously cited in which he expressed alarm at the militarization of American foreign policy and at coordinated NATO efforts to "control" zones outside European boundaries. Calling US policy dangerous and irresponsible, *Krasnaia zvezda* accused Washington of seeking to widen the Gulf War by creating an arms dependency in the region:

> It is this dependence which Washington is seeking to use in order to draw the Arab countries into the Iran–Iraq conflict and to heat the situation in the region to the utmost with a view to implementing its hegemonistic plans. It is operating in several directions. First, the Arab rulers are in every way intimidated with "the growth to the military threat" from Iran and with "Islamic revolutionary actions of the Iranian type" in the Arab countries themselves. In other words, it is recommended that they perceive as an enemy not only Iran but also the national-patriotic forces in their own countries and to prepare for reprisals against them.[48]

Moreover, the Soviets repeated that, in the words of one *Izvestiia* columnist: "We are not indifferent to what is happening in a region so close to our borders."[49] And, a statement issued at a meeting of Arab communist parties reiterated Soviet alarm. The communique charged that US activities were designed "to weaken the national patriotic forces in the region . . . and pose a threat to the Soviet Union from the South." The statement concluded that it was, therefore, necessary to end the Iran–Iraq War immediately.[50]

Interestingly, the significant widening of the war coincided with intensified diplomatic maneuvering. On June 12, both sides announced that they had accepted a UN-mediated moratorium on the bombing of civilian targets. Nonetheless, Iran and Iraq rejected any suggestions that the bombing halt might portend an end to the war. In fact, both sides sought additional weaponry. Iraq announced that it had taken delivery of two new types of air-to-surface missiles, and on June 4, an Iranian delegation led by Sayyid Muhammed Sadr, director general of the foreign ministry, arrived in Moscow. During the meetings with Andrei Gromyko, the Soviets expressed their desire to have "friendly" relations with Teheran. Western press reports added that Iran might have been interested in procuring additional Soviet arms.[51]

During this period, Soviet broadcasts beamed at Iran were clearly directed at fostering better links to Teheran. It should be remembered that the USSR possessed a major economic stake in cordial relations with Teheran. The disruption in gas sales had created imbalances; thus, around the anniversary of the original gas pipeline agreement, Soviet propaganda outlets released Farsi commentaries which noted the extensive Soviet assistance and contribution to the Iranian economy and the consequent losses to Iranian development. The pricing differences which precipitated the rupture in the agreement were attributed to the "unfriendly views" of former officials. Almost simultaneously, the Soviets "advertised" other forms of assistance to Iran. For example, one commentary explained the nature and growth of the cargo transit agreement between the two countries. The transshipment of Iranian cargoes overland across the USSR was said to aid Iran in its anti-imperialist battles and also to be an example of what truly friendly, mutually beneficial relations would bring.[52] Taking credit for helping Iran resist imperialist pressures, the USSR seemingly advertised the successes achieved with Soviet economic assistance.

Soviet officials implemented the well orchestrated propaganda campaign outlined above at the same time as they withdrew Soviet energy experts from Iran because of intense fighting in the Ahwaz area. Unfortunately for the Iranians, Soviet technicians left a major power plant unfinished. Equally unfortunate for the Soviets, the withdrawal left the USSR vulnerable to propaganda attacks by Teheran. In turn, Moscow charged Iranian spokesmen with attempting to incite anti-Soviet sentiments among the population. Hence, the war dimmed Soviet prospects for the utilization of economic assistance and trade relations as foreign policy tools to halt the deterioration in Soviet–Iranian relations. Contemporaneously, the deterioration itself became more pronounced. As leader of "progressive" forces, the USSR could not let a second wave of trials of Tudeh activists pass unnoticed. Yet, *Pravda* contained Tudeh statements condemning the trials and not formal Soviet governmental protests. Farsi broadcasts to Teheran, as might be expected, extolled the Tudeh's patriotism and role in the 1979 revolution. Thus, despite the exchanges of delegations and the praise for Soviet-aided development projects, other trends in Iran rendered Moscow less then sanguine about the prospects for better relations.

Because of the disappointing events in Iran and the course of the war itself, Moscow evidenced an even more pronounced tilt to Iraq by the fall of 1984. Several articles openly sided with Iraq, while condemning ruling circles in Iran for refusing mediation and for continuing the war effort. In July, the Kuwait news agency reported an interview with Troyanovskii in which he seemed to justify the Iraqi attacks on Kharg Island as being "within the framework" of the war.[53] In October, Tariq Aziz met in the Kremlin with Soviet leaders. In what was billed as a working visit, the Iraqis and Soviets discussed the Palestinian question and, of course, the Iran–Iraq War. According to the TASS dispatch, Aziz praised Soviet stands on international issues; however, the report omitted any mention of agreement on the war or Iraqi policies. The talks were described as both "friendly" and "frank."[54]

Problems persisted, however. In November, Baghdad reestablished diplomatic relations with the US. This was but a further indication of the Iraqi desire to distance itself from the Kremlin. Soviet observers spent considerable energies to downplay the potentially changing regional alignments. Foreign affairs analysts portrayed Iraq as a peacemaker and one writer included the following quotation from an Iraqi official in his coverage of the war. "I wish to stress that this [diplomatic relations between the US and Iraq] is an act of normalization of state relations. But it does not mean any rapprochement or coincidence in the viewpoints of Washington and Baghdad."[55] In general, the Soviets repeatedly expressed their concern that the war facilitated US penetration of the region and urged clerical circles in Teheran to put an end to the fighting. Their "sell" was directed at the alleged community of interests among all in the region to avoid foreign military intervention. Moscow also appeared to try to convince the Iranians that they were vulnerable to imperialist interference as long as the war raged. All of these themes fell on deaf ears. Thus, at the end of 1984, Soviet problems with Iran and the continuing coolness of relations with Iraq indicated that the prolongation of the war was to the USSR a losing proposition.

Notes

1. Tareq Y. Ismael, *Iraq and Iran: Roots of Conflict* (Syracuse: Syracuse University Press, 1982), p. 5.

2. See the discussion in Lenore G. Martin, *The Unstable Gulf, Threats From Within* (Lexington, MA: Lexington Books, 1984), pp. 36, 37.

3. Robert O. Freedman, *Soviet Policy Toward the Middle East Since 1970* (Third edition), (New York: Praeger Publishers, 1982), p. 75.

4. *Pravda* and *Izvestiia*, February 18, 1972, p. 1, 4 in *Current Digest of the Soviet Press* (hereafter *CDSP*), Vol. XXIV, No. 7, March 15, 1972, p. 8.

5. Alvin Z. Rubinstein, *Soviet Policy Toward Turkey, Iran, and Afghanistan* (New York: Praeger Publishers, 1982), p. 76.

6. "On a Friendly Visit," *Pravda*, November 19, 1974, pp. 1, 4 in *CDSP*, Vol. XXVI, No. 47, December 18, 1974, p. 17.

7. Nadav Safran, *Saudi Arabia: The Quest for Stability* (Cambridge: Harvard University Press, 1985), see especially chapter 10.

8. A. Ostalsky, "Who Needs the War," *Komsomolskaia Pravda*, October 25, 1980, p. 3, in *CDSP*, Vol. XXXII, No. 44, December 3, 1980, p. 1; and V. Matveyev, "Danger Signals," *Izvestiia*, October 1, 1980, p. 4, in *CDSP*, Vol. XXXII, No. 39, October 29, 1980, pp. 2–3.

9. L. Medvedko, "The Persian Gulf: A Revival of Gunboat Diplomacy," *International Affairs*, No. 12, p. 26.

10. *Pravda*, December 9, 1980, pp. 1, 2, in *Foreign Broadcast Information Service, Soviet Union Daily Report* (hereafter *FBIS SOV*), 80 240, December 11, 1980, p. D7.

11. Claudia Wright, "Implications of the Iraq–Iran War," *Foreign Affairs*, Vol. 59, No. 2 (Winter 1980/81), p. 289.

12. Avi Plascov, "Strategic Developments in the Persian Gulf," *Middle East Contemporary Survey,* Volume Five (1980–1981) (New York: Holmes and Meier Publishers, Inc., 1982), p. 26.

13. Bruce Porter, "Soviet Arms and the Iraqi–Iranian Conflict," *Radio Liberty Research,* RL 382/80, October 16, 1980.

14. TASS, April 23, 1981, in *FBIS SOV* 81 079, April 24, 1981, p. H7.

15. William Quandt, *Saudi Arabia in the 1980s, Foreign Policy, Security, and Oil* (Washington: Brookings Institution, 1981) p. 21.

16. TASS, October 8, 1980, *FBIS SOV* 80 198, October 9, 1980, p. H2.

17. Shahram Chubin, "The Soviet Union and Iran," *Foreign Affairs,* Vol. 61, No. 4 (Spring 1983), p. 934.

18. See, for example, the discussion in Safran, *Saudi Arabia,* p. 366ff.

19. *Pravda,* March 2, 1981, p. 4.

20. *Pravda,* April 11, 1981, p. 2.

21. *Washington Post,* April 19, 1981, pp. A1, A20.

22. Pavel Demchenko, "USSR–Iran: In the Interests of Good Neighborliness," *Pravda,* March 9, 1982, p. 4.

23. Yuri Glukhov, "Will the Conflict Be Extinguished?" *Pravda,* May 31, 1982, p. 6 and Igor Beliaev, "Persian Gulf: Second Hot War Who Benefits?" *Literaturnaia gazeta,* July 21, 1982, p. 9.

24. Michael Getler, "Gulf Area Maneuvers Possible," *Washington Post,* July 17, 1982, pp. A1, A14.

25. Moscow Radio Peace and Progress, April 9, 1982, *FBIS SOV* 82 071, April 13, 1982, p. H4.

26. Volinskii (8th in a series), Moscow in Persian, October 15, 1982, *FBIS SOV* 82 201, October 18, 1982, p. H8.

27. Drew Middleton, "Iraq Says its Treaty with the Soviets Hasn't Worked," *New York Times,* November 17, 1982, p. A3.

28. Ofra Bengio, "Iraq," *Middle East Contemporary Survey,* Volume Six (1981–1982) (New York: Holmes and Meier Publishers, Inc., 1984), p. 607.

29. Drew Middleton, "New Iraqi Strategy is Seen in War with Iran," *New York Times,* October 31, 1982, p. 6.

30. *Al Watan* October 30, 1982, p. 17, *FBIS SOV* 82 214, November 4, 1982, p. CC4.

31. Moscow in Persian, October 22, 1982, *FBIS SOV* 82 207, October 26, 1982, p. H12.

32. V. Gudev, "An Unnecessary and Dangerous Conflict," *New Times,* No. 47, November 19, 1982, pp. 26–27.

33. Dmitri Volsky, "Talk With a Reader," *Novoe Vremia,* No. 41, October 8, 1982, p. 31 in *FBIS SOV* 82 201, October 18, 1982, p. H8.

34. See KUNA, December 11, 1982, in *Foreign Broadcast Information Service, Middle East* (hereafter *FBIS MEA*) 82 240, December 14, 1982, p. E1.

35. Igor Sheftunov commentary, Moscow in Persian, November 19, 1982, *FBIS SOV* 82 225, November 22, 1985, pp. H7–8.

36. *Pravda,* "Against the National Interests of Iran," February 19, 1983, p. 4.

37. *Pravda,* "Concerning the Anti-Soviet Campaign in Iran," May 6, 1983, p. 4.

38. See, for example, broadcast May 29, 1983, *FBIS SOV* 83 108, June 3, 1983, p. H4.

39. *Pravda,* June 17, 1983, italics added.

40. *Nedelia,* No. 41, October 1983, p. 9 in *FBIS SOV* 83 207, October 25, 1983, p. 5.

41. A. Omin, "Who Is Stirring Up the Waters in the Persian Gulf?" *Izvestiia,* October 24, 1983, p. 5.

42. Evgeny Primakov, "USA: Policy of Destabilization in the Middle East," *International Affairs,* March, 1984, p. 39.

43. February 25, 1984, *FBIS SOV* 84 039, February 27, 1984, p. CC19.

44. *Pravda,* March 7, 1984, p. 8.

45. *Pravda,* April 26, 1984, p. 1.

46. Col. D. Ivanov, "In Another's Voice," *Krasnaia zvezda,* March 22, 1984, p. 3 in *FBIS SOV* 84 060, March 27, 1984, p. H6.

47. TASS, June 9, 1984, *FBIS SOV* 84 113, June 11, 1984, pp. H2-3.

48. V. Pustov, "Interference Under the Guise of Aid," *Krasnaia zvezda,* July 1, 1984, p. 3.

49. V. Matveyev, "Political Observer's Opinion," *Izvestiia,* June 10, 1984, pp. 4-5.

50. "Statement by Arab Countries' Communist and Workers Parties," *Pravda,* June 19, 1984, p. 4.

51. Dusko Doder, "Iranians End Fence Mending Trip," *Washington Post,* June 8, 1984, p. A28.

52. Broadcast, November 14, 1984, *FBIS SOV* 84 222, November 15, 1984, p. H2.

53. KUNA, July 3, 1984, *FBIS SOV* 84 130, July 4, 1984, pp. H2-3.

54. TASS, October 19, 1984, *FBIS SOV* 84 205, October 22, 1984, p. H1.

55. Interview with L. N. Jasim, minister of information of Iraq, *Za Rubezhom,* No. 4, January 1985, pp. 12-13, *FBIS SOV* 85 017, January 25, 1985, p. H2.

3

Gorbachev and the Iran-Iraq War

Political Succession

It would not be an exaggeration to say that between Leonid Brezhnev's death in November 1982 and Mikhail Gorbachev's accession to
power in March 1985 the Soviet Union was preoccupied with the
prolonged succession crisis. Yuri Andropov's elevation to General Secretary brought with it a short-lived attempt to cut Soviet costs in the
Third World. His brief tenure in office also produced a pronounced
deterioration in Soviet–American relations when the Soviets walked
out of arms negotiation talks. Following his death in February 1984,
Konstantin Chernenko, a Brezhnev protege, assumed power. Like his
immediate predecessor, he became ill in office and died following a
long absence from the scene. Finally, in March 1985, Mikhail Gorbachev was appointed General Secretary. That there were three leadership transitions in two-and-one-half years meant that Soviet foreign
policy drifted. With few exceptions, the outlines of Soviet–Third World
relations remained unchanged. The same held true for the Iran–Iraq
War. The decisions made between 1980 and 1982 could not easily be
undone. As noted in the previous chapter, under Andropov and Chernenko, Soviet policy basically stayed within the already established
framework.

Mikhail Gorbachev brought to the Politburo new ideas and new
energies. Clearly determined to revitalize the Soviet system, he shifted
significant numbers of party personnel and introduced new forms of
labor discipline. At the same time, Gorbachev cracked down on the
rampant alcoholism in the Soviet Union and urged managers and
workers alike to take initiatives and generally to work harder. He further
sought to reverse the USSR's economic decline by introducing *peres-
troika* (restructuring) and *glasnost'* (openness).

Gorbachev's campaign for change touched the foreign policy realm
as well. Personnel changes included the replacement of Andrei Gro-

myko, the long-time foreign minister, with Georgian Eduard Shevardnadze. Although Gromyko was an early Gorbachev supporter—he offered the nominating speech at the Politburo meeting at which Gorbachev
was named—his elevation to the ceremonial post of president allowed
Gorbachev much greater flexibility in foreign policy. Specifically, Gromyko was associated with several long-term policies in the Middle East
and his replacement, therefore, allowed Gorbachev to try out new
approaches. Shevardnadze's inexperience in foreign policy permitted the
new general secretary a free hand with which to mould Soviet foreign
policy and his appearance and polish facilitated a new Soviet image
abroad. Another significant shift occurred in the party's international
department. Anatoly Dobrynin was brought home from Washington to
supplant the aged Boris Ponomarev. This change reflected Gorbachev's
new agenda: the primacy of the US–Soviet relationship.

Unlike his major predecessor Leonid Brezhnev, Gorbachev felt that
the Third World was a relatively low priority. A comparison of the
two general secretaries' speeches at the twenty-sixth and twenty-seventh
party congresses strikingly reveals the differences. Whereas Brezhnev
would wax poetic about Soviet successes in the Third World, Gorbachev
devoted only a few lines to the Third World at all. This worried several
Third World figures who in their speeches sought to remind the general
secretary of their importance to the USSR. This is not to say that the
Soviet Union would willingly relinquish what it has achieved over the
post-war period. Indeed, Gorbachev has shown a willingness to take
risks to aid clients in trouble. By the same token, he has also demonstrated a willingness to try to cut his losses. In his speech to the
twenty-seventh congress of the CPSU, Gorbachev referred to Afghanistan as a "bleeding sore" and signalled that he sought ways to extricate
the Soviet Union from the prolonged counterinsurgency struggle there.
By April 1988, the USSR, the US, Pakistan, and the Soviet-supported
Kabul regime signed an agreement which would terminate the direct
Soviet intervention in Afghanistan. Gorbachev has also demonstrated
an increased flexibility toward the rest of Asia and the Middle East.
With his 1986 Vladivostok speech, he made overtures to Japan, China,
and the Association of Southeast Asian Nations. Additionally, with
behind-the-scenes contacts with Israeli officials, the USSR seemed to
move toward a new role in the Arab–Israeli dispute (see Chapter 4).
All told, Gorbachev clearly hopes to direct Soviet energies to more
productive and potentially positive endeavors. At the least, the Soviets
could then turn their full attention to other dangers in the Third World,
including the Gulf War.

Gorbachev's First Year

The beginning of 1985 appeared to be a replay of 1984. Soviet relations with Teheran alternated between condemnations of Iranian domestic affairs and of Iranian refusals to consider negotiation, and exchanges of several diplomatic and economic delegations. Concomitantly, the Kremlin's relations with Iraq remained cool but stable. Arms shipments continued, as did delegational exchanges. On February 20, the USSR and Iraq signed an intergovernmental agreement on oil development and on April 9 a cultural accord was initialed.

On the battle front, the fighting between Iran and Iraq continued as it had before with periodic offensives and counteroffensives as well as with attacks on neutral shipping in the Gulf. Moscow proved to be watching events in the Gulf carefully. Communiques from the front were included in TASS dispatches, but the Kremlin issued no analyses or commentary. Then, March 1985 witnessed the most intense hostilities of the then four-and-one-half-year-old Gulf War. Iraq seemingly provoked this round of fighting with the hopes of forcing Iran to accept a mediated settlement. Breaking the almost nine-month-old moratorium on the bombardment of civilian centers, Iraq attacked areas in Iran and the Iranians retaliated by bombing Basra. On March 11, the two combatants attacked each other's capitals. Then, on March 12, the Iranians launched a major offensive toward the Baghdad-to-Basra highway. They progressed to within six miles of the road. Within a week, Iraq counterattacked successfully, forcing the Iranians to withdraw. Iraqi activities included significant strikes at the oil facilities at Kharg Island.

Moscow's response to the intensified fighting was predictable. Repeatedly proclaiming its neutrality, the USSR renewed its call for an end to the war. It is entirely possible that the Iraqi-induced escalation added to the tensions in Soviet–Iraqi relations. The strain becomes evident when one considers the press coverage given to a trip made by Tariq Aziz to Moscow. *Pravda* mentioned the visit only briefly on page four of the edition of March 31, 1985. It was called a working visit and there was none of the usual commentary characterizing the "atmospherics" of the meetings.[1] At the time of the thirteenth anniversary of the Friendship and Cooperation Treaty, Moscow expressed "confidence" that relations between the Kremlin and Iraq, "firmly established by this treaty, will develop further . . ." This was hardly an effusive greeting to send to Baghdad.[2]

Despite the dissatisfaction with Iraqi policy, the overall themes in Soviet editorials and press commentaries about the escalation were not new. What was different were the strident criticisms of Iran. One *Pravda* dispatch, written by chief Middle East correspondent Yuri Glukhov, claimed that Iran squandered its wealth on the war.[3] In an interesting review, *Krasnaia zvezda* concluded that Iran's March offensive was unproductive. Citing the relative parity of ground forces, the author underscored that Iraq possessed superior air equipment and total power. Ironically, almost simultaneously reports appeared in the Western press that Iran was using, as well, Soviet-made SCUD missiles which they had captured from Iraq in an earlier offensive.[4] Most scathingly, the *Krasnaia zvezda* article noted that the militarist campaign and battlefield operations, which were based on "Muslim Shi'ite extremism," have "reaffirmed that religious fanaticism cannot replace military training and much else needed in war."[5]

Following the month of intense fighting, the Iranian deputy foreign minister arrived in Moscow. One result of the meeting was the scheduling of an economic ministers' meeting for June. Most interesting was a report by the Kuwaiti news agency that Iran had asked the Soviet Union to intercede with Iraq not to use Soviet-built long range missiles.[6] This would seem to indicate not only that the Iraqi attacks were having the desired effect, but also that in the Iranian view the USSR could influence the decisions made in Baghdad.

As the war continued throughout the spring and summer, there was considerable diplomatic maneuvering and an intensified search for arms. In May, the Kremlin hosted a delegation from the Arab League which went to Moscow to discuss the situation in the Gulf. Gromyko used the meeting to reiterate Soviet public neutrality, and, of course, support for the Palestinians. Nonetheless, the exchanges were described as "frank." Tariq Aziz was a member of the delegation and held separate talks with Gromyko at the time. Presumably, the subject of more Soviet arms for Iraq was broached. In June, Moscow was the site of a meeting of the Soviet–Iraqi committee on technological and economic cooperation, and at the end of the month, President Saddam Hussein met with the Soviet ambassador in Baghdad. The Iraqi and Soviet maritime delegations met in August and Moscow hosted a week-long celebration of Iraqi–Soviet friendship.

The Iranians were also on the go in June. Prime Minister Rafsanjani's itinerary included Libya, Syria, and the PRC. The first two, of course, are primary supporters and suppliers of the Teheran government. China represented a potential new source of diplomatic support and arms. TASS reported that the Iranian official received the "go-ahead" for military cooperation with China, in return for oil.[7] According to Western reports, China agreed to sell Iran J6 fighters, a Chinese version of the MiG 21, T59 tanks, heavy artillery, multiple rocket launchers and surface-to-air missiles.[8]

July saw a renewed Iranian offensive in the northern sector which the Iraqis claimed to have repulsed. In the face of the intensified hostilities, Moscow withdrew more of its advisors from Iran. As they had a year earlier, the Soviets felt the need to defend their actions in radio broadcasts to Iran. Following Gromyko's elevation to the presidency of the USSR, Moscow displayed a slight increase in the flexibility of its policy toward Iran. In contrast to Gromyko's policy of "reciprocity," Soviet–Iranian economic relations received a boost, despite the exodus of Soviet personnel. Representatives of the Iranian chamber of commerce visited Moscow to discuss mining and industrial development. Then, Iraq again attacked Kharg Island in a renewed attempt to cut off Iranian foreign earnings. In retaliation, Iran launched a major attack in the central sector. This by now periodic escalation of hostilities found the Soviets condemning the war and playing their usual careful balancing act. Again Moscow blasted Iran for continuing the war. In an interesting television broadcast, Aleksandr Bovin characterized the war as a tactic used by Iran to alleviate domestic discontent. He further criticized Iranian politics, labelling the regime "theocratic and despotic."[9] This domestic commentary stands in marked contrast to reports which indicated that Iran was importing weapons through Soviet territory.[10]

Soviet–Iranian economic contacts continued throughout the fall. The long-planned meeting of economic delegations finally took place in Moscow in September. Both sides proclaimed the usefulness of the talks and hopes for further economic cooperation. Soviet Farsi broadcasts in the period touted Soviet economic assistance to Iran and support for Teheran's anti-imperialism.

September was, of course, the fifth anniversary of the war. Soviet commentary was surprisingly sparse. Thematically, Soviet propaganda remained unchanged: Continuing hostilities benefit only imperialism and Zionism and not either combatant. A broadcast to Iran stressed that recent Iranian offensives had brought only additional destruction. The commentary suggested that:

This war is actually stalemated now. Therefore, what are the goals of this meaningless war and fratricide? What serious reason can be given to explain why this war . . . must continue? There are enough facts to prove that there is not a single difference between Iran and Iraq that cannot be solved peacefully through talks if both sides show good will and statesmanship. Political foresight and insight, the careful consideration of objective facts, and the avoidance of ambitious presumptuousness, which has reached the point of intervention in the domestic affairs of another country, are elements that can help Iran and Iraq break the stalemate of war and bloodshed.[11]

As the diplomatic record indicates, the Soviets had to date managed to maintain rather tenuous ties with both sides. By the same token, if they had hoped to cultivate Khomeini's anti-Americanism through their initial tilt toward Iran, they did not succeed. Although the door to Iran wasn't closed completely, relations were clearly strained by the Ayatollah's rhetorical anti-Sovietism and his policy of exporting the fundamentalist revolution. The pattern of criticism of Teheran's policies alternating with attempts to reopen economic relations continued. The summer of 1985 may well be the one slight variation in the established pattern. The Soviet overtures to Iran were coupled with what may be considered the proverbial toe in the door, arms transshipped from Libya and Syria. Indeed, it was reported in September 1985 that Iran had taken delivery of 130 Soviet missiles through Syria, and in this case, North Korea.

As for Iraq, the Soviets appeared to be biding their time, taking what crumbs they could get. Relations were generally cool, although economic delegations travelled and cooperative agreements were signed. Iraq continued to diversify its military supply with purchases from the French in particular. In September, the Iraqis purchased forty-five US-made helicopters and in December, *Al Qabas* reported Iraqi acquisition of newly-developed French missiles which were purported to be superior to the exocets.[12] It would not be until Saddam Hussein's trip to Moscow in December that a change in Soviet–Iraqi relations would occur.

The trip in mid-December represented Saddam Hussein's first trip to the USSR since acceding to the presidency of Iraq. According to TASS, talks between Gorbachev and Hussein were conducted in a "businesslike, frank, and friendly atmosphere."[13] In the esoteric language of the Kremlin, this characterization would indicate some agreements and some major disagreements between Baghdad and Moscow. As is the custom for state visits such as this, *Pravda* reported the speeches given by now-President Gromyko and Hussein at the Kremlin reception. It is interesting to note that *Pravda* provided a verbatim copy of Saddam's speech except for discussion of the Gulf War. The party daily wrote: "The president went on to *dwell* on the Iran–Iraq War. He reaffirmed Iraq's desire to settle the conflict by peaceful means. . . ."[14] Baghdad radio, in contrast, quoted the text of President Hussein's statements:

> The other problem from which the region is suffering is the Iranian regime's insistence on continuing the expansionist war of aggression against Iraq. . . .

The Teheran rulers' insistence on continuing the war and rejecting
international resolution and initiatives, which call for solving the dispute
by peaceful means on the basis of inernational law, exposes the region
to grave dangers and certainly serves the Zionist and imperialist aims.[15]

Aside from the name calling, there is nothing in the speech about
which the Kremlin could disagree.

The Soviets for their part wanted to present all their basic international positions in the forum provided by the Hussein reception.
Andrei Gromyko's dinner speech seemed to reflect the list of Soviet
foreign policy priorities: prevention of nuclear war, praise for the November 1985 summit meeting with President Ronald Reagan, prevention of the militarization of space, an international conference to deal
with the Arab–Israeli dispute, and finally the Gulf War. Following the
usual proclamation of neutrality, Gromyko said: "In our view, those
who contrary to all logic, call for the war to be continued 'to a victorious
end' and who regard it as a means of settling scores with the enemy
and imposing their political will on him, are acting unreasonably."[16]

The regional presses provided a glimpse of how the visit was seen
by the Iraqis and others. Baghdad media cited the "strands of friendship
and cooperation" as well as emphasized that the Soviets considered
the trip a new development in Soviet–Iraqi friendship.[17] Some of the
most interesting analyses came from an interview with Taha Yasin
Ramadan which appeared in the *Jordan Times*. Mr. Ramadan was
quoted as saying that Saddam Hussein's trip to the USSR was successful
but that Iraqi "relations with the Soviet Union are still below our
expectations." He added, however, that Baghdad and Moscow hold
similar views of "Iran's aggressive policies." Obviously, one of Iraq's
major concerns would be securing additional arms supplies, and reports
surfaced that Hussein had indeed requested new arms shipments. In
the same interview, Ramadan was described as "very satisfied with the
results of last week's talks [Hussein in Moscow] concerning [Iraq's]
need for weapons."[18] Simultaneously, the Qataris and Kuwaitis indicated
that in the aftermath of Hussein's trip to Moscow, Iraq would receive
weapons it did not have in its arsenal previously.[19]

Thus 1985 and the first ten months of the Gorbachev era ended on
a note of outreach to Iraq. As this analysis indicated, the Saddam
Hussein trip represented somewhat of a thaw in Soviet–Iraqi relations.
Yet, Moscow clearly had not given up hope of cultivating the Iranian
leadership. In 1986, the previously established pattern continued: The
USSR alternately condemned Iranian domestic developments and pur-
sued increased economic and political contacts. For example, a *New
Times* article entitled "The Iranian Scene" claimed that the regime in

Teheran had implemented no reforms to benefit the people since the revolution. Its author further criticized Iran for continuing the Gulf War, for exporting the Islamic revolution, and for aiding the Afghan mujaheedin.[20] The same week Gorbachev sent a message to the Islamic regime through the Soviet ambassador in Teheran. As a follow-up, Ambassador Boldyrev met with the Iranian deputy foreign minister to discuss Soviet–Iranian cooperative relations. These intensified contacts culminated in the trip of Soviet deputy foreign minister Georgii Kornienko to Teheran. While there, he met with Velayati and Rafsanjani. According to Iranian dispatches, the discussions were "extensive" and Kornienko emphasized Soviet interest in expanding relations between Moscow and Teheran.

Middle East sources revealed that the Soviet–Iranian discussions laid the groundwork for further economic talks between Konstantin Katushev, head of the state committee for foreign economic relations and Muhammad Javad Iravani, minister for economy and finance. One of the major issues on the economic agenda was to be the resumption of Iranian gas exports to the USSR.[21] Ironically, while the economic thrust of these sessions was clearly in Soviet interests, the Kremlin provided no commentary or even announcement of the meetings. The Iranian reportage would seem to indicate that Teheran wanted to put on the Soviets' best face; yet, it would seem fair to conclude from the absence of Soviet dispatches that Moscow was displeased with the results of the talks. Despite the hint of improvement in mutual economic relations, the Iranian position on the war remained unchanged. The Soviets still had to contend with the spillover from the war in terms of the American presence in the region and in terms of fissures within the Arab world.

It is entirely possible that this 1986 renewal of contacts was designed by Teheran. Iranian reports all indicated that Kornienko travelled to Iran at Iranian invitation. Although a new natural gas deal and further economic contacts would be mutually beneficial, Teheran may have hoped to convince Moscow of the importance of improved relations. Indeed, the promise of natural gas sales, an oil deal, or a more secure relationship between the two neighbors may have been dangled in front of the Soviets in return for a limitation on the Soviet arms shipped directly to Iraq. Further evidence for this line of reasoning may be gathered from the timing of the February 1986 Fao offensive. Iranian revolutionary guards and volunteers successfully crossed the Shatt-al-Arab and staged a landing on the Fao Peninsula. The attack caught the Iraqis, who were expecting a major offensive toward Basra, by surprise. The Iraqi Air Force was unable to destroy Iran's main pontoon bridge and the wet terrain was unsuited for tanks. With supplies and additional manpower (estimated at some 30,000 troops), the Iranians held onto Fao until the spring of 1988.

In some ways the Fao offensive put the USSR on the defensive. Moscow's propaganda condemned the intensifying hostilities and claimed as usual that the widening conflict benefited only the imperialists and Zionists. TASS claimed on March 19 that the US threatened to intervene militarily in the escalating conflict, and added: "It is understandable, however, that the true motives of the United States' actions are not in helping the Persian Gulf states, but in asserting and consolidating its presence in this strategically important area of the world."[22]

With the resulting widespread fear of an Iranian breakthrough in the Gulf War, the Soviets somehow had to come to the Iraqis' aid. On February 17, Tariq Aziz went to Moscow to meet with his Soviet counterpart. During the talks, Shevardnadze expressed Soviet concern over the growing military conflict. In addition, faced with the Iranian offensive, the Soviets apparently felt constrained to deny allegations that they were aiding the Iranian effort militarily. Of course, the typical propaganda proclaimed Soviet neutrality. But when asked about specific deliveries, Evgenii Primakov refused to answer questions about East European transfers to Iran. And, Aleksandr Kiselev, head of the department of US Middle East policy studies in the Institute for the Study of the USA and Canada, responded in the same interview:

> When Iraq was occupying Iranian territory there was grumbling against the Soviet Union because of its decision to stop giving arms to Iraq with whom it has a treaty of friendship. But now no such grumbling is being heard. Why? Because it is now Iran that is occupying Iraqi territory.
>
> We support Iraq because it wants a peaceful settlement while Iran is rejecting it.[23]

The next month, Soviet–Iraqi contacts continued with a visit to Moscow by Ramadan. In light of the long-term occupation of Fao, it would seem fair to conclude that Ramadan travelled to the USSR to request additional Soviet support. Indeed, the Soviet reports of the visit stressed that both sides were interested in furthering and strengthening "mutually beneficial economic, scientific, and technological cooperation."[24] The latter may refer to military and logistical support.

Change in the Kremlin and in the Gulf

Since Mikhail Gorbachev's accession to power, Soviet priorities have shifted to domestic concerns. The new Soviet leadership is clearly interested in revitalizing the ailing Soviet economy and shaking up the stodgy bureaucracy. In addition, if one can judge from his speech at the twenty-seventh party congress, Gorbachev is far less concerned with the Third World than were his predecessors. This does not mean diminished interest in the Gulf, which is so geographically close to the USSR, but it may well mean a different way of dealing with Iran or Iraq. The combination of the reordering of foreign policy concerns and of the setting of the economy as top priority is reflected in intensified economic activity with each of the combatants.

In the spring of 1986, there occurred an explosion of economic contacts with both Baghdad and Teheran. A flurry of economic exchanges followed Ramadan's trip to Moscow. In early May, a Soviet technical delegation went to Baghdad to prepare for the May 19 meeting of the heads of the joint Soviet-Iraqi committee for economic, scientific, and technical cooperation. The discussion resulted in the signing of several contracts and netted a meeting between Konstantin Katushev and Saddam Hussein. According to reports, the two signed an agreement by which the Soviets would build the first stage of a cross-country pipeline and they initialed a five-year economic cooperation treaty. These talks between the USSR and Iraq were described as having taken place in an atmosphere of "businesslike cooperation and mutual understanding."[25]

Of course, these enhanced contacts with Baghdad were balanced, if not outweighed, by the almost simultaneous Soviet initiatives toward Iran. In June, the director general of the Soviet state commission on economic and international cooperation for Asia and the Middle East met with Muhammad Javad Larijani, the Iranian deputy foreign minister for international and economic affairs. At the same time as economic negotiations intensified, Mikhail Gorbachev sent a message to President Khamene'i. It is interesting to note that the text of the message was not revealed, nor was it reported in the Soviet press. The meeting was the opening shot in a summertime flurry of exchanges and negotiations that was to be interrupted only temporarily by the Iranian seizure of two Soviet ships in September. By August, when Larijani met in Moscow with Gromyko and Shevardnadze, both sides were openly speaking of the desire to better relations. The discussions, which were described as "frank" and "businesslike," (indicating disagreements) produced an announcement that the permanent Iranian–Soviet commission would convene before the end of the year.

Two weeks later Nikolai Ryzhkov met with Iran's oil minister, Gholam Reza Aqazadeh. The two declared that the differences in their countries' respective social systems should not preclude productive relations between them. Most important, the August 19th meeting resulted in an agreement to resume Iranian natural gas deliveries to the USSR. The deal followed Soviet agreement to reduce its oil exports to Western Europe by 100,000 barrels a day. That move had been made at Iranian request. According to Western reports at the time, Teheran was scheduled to supply the USSR with 105 million cubic feet of gas beginning in December 1986.[26] The resumption of natural gas shipments to the Soviet Union would alleviate some logistical problems experienced by Moscow in supplying its southern regions. Moreover, from the Iranian perspective, the deal would ease Teheran's isolation and would provide additional hard currency earnings to the troubled Iranian economy. Finally, the negotiations represent a major push to improve Soviet–Iranian relations and to repay the Soviets for agreeing to reduce oil deliveries to the West.[27]

Despite the seizure of the Soviet ships, an event which both sides downplayed, further contacts occurred in September. The most important of these was a meeting in Teheran of the Iranian–Soviet chamber of commerce. Following the discussions, both sides again issued positive appraisals of the talks and stressed the need to promote more links in the interests of both countries. Then in October, Gromyko received the newly-appointed Iranian ambassador to Moscow. At the time the Soviet press underscored the Kremlin's concern regarding anti-Soviet propaganda in Iran. Yet, the Iranian press disclosed that Gromyko said that Soviet specialists would soon return to Iran. It had earlier been reported that Soviet experts would go to Iran to examine the state of the gas pipeline. Here again the ambiguous nature of Soviet–Iranian relations can be seen. On the one hand, the Kremlin pursued renewed economic contacts, while on the other hand, it remained worried about the anti-Soviet tenor of politics in Teheran.

The revelations that the US had sold arms to Teheran—Irangate—provided Moscow with a tremendous propaganda opportunity; yet, they also clearly alarmed the Kremlin. Soviet statements, press dispatches, and broadcasts beamed to the Middle East all emphasized the duplicitous nature of US foreign policy. Moscow attempted to portray itself as the true friend of the Arabs, while discrediting American statements about neutrality in the Iran–Iraq War. Because the disclosures sent such shock waves through the Arab world, the Soviets felt constrained, yet again, to deny reports that they too were dealing arms to the Iranians. Underneath the bravado, however, lay a very real concern that Iran might indeed reestablish diplomatic relations with the United States. As unsuccessful as the Soviet Union had been in cultivating the Khomeini regime, it could at least draw comfort from the fact that until the November 1986 revelations, there were few known contacts between Teheran and Washington. Igor Beliaev, the *Literaturnaia gazeta* correspondent, charged that Reagan wanted to turn Teheran into an anti-Soviet bridgehead. He added that the US's goal was "the resumption of everything that was done against the Soviet Union until February 1979. . . ."[28] The US arms sales to Teheran, including TOW and Hawk missiles, notwithstanding, Soviet–Iranian negotiations continued. With praise for the Iranians for pursuing a neighborly policy, the Soviets met with their Iranian counterparts to convene the tenth meeting of the standing commission. In recess since 1980, the commission's meeting had been long promised. The discussions netted a new protocol on economic relations and it seemed as if neither side wanted to let the arms sales divert its attention from what could become again a valuable trade relationship.

The Soviet concern regarding the US's role in the region has been a constant theme in Soviet policy toward the Gulf. It should be recalled that Moscow blamed the US for the war, tried to utilize the hostage crisis to promote anti-Americanism, and continually attempted to forestall the acceptability of an American presence in the region. With the background of the disclosures regarding "Irangate," Gorbachev used the platform of the Indian parliament to reiterate Soviet proposals for the demilitarization of the Gulf. While on a successful state visit to India, the general secretary proposed:

1. to reduce the size and activities of naval forces in the Indian Ocean.
2. to negotiate with the US and Asian countries on confidence-building measures.
3. to pursue multinational negotiations to guarantee sea lanes.
4. to promote air traffic safety in the region.
5. to draft a treaty to combat terrorism.[29]

These proposals were clearly reminiscent of Brezhnev's 1980 offer to demilitarize the Indian Ocean and Persian Gulf.

If the emphasis in the fall of 1986 was on relations with Iran, it was because Soviet–Iraqi relations were relatively quiescent. There were several delegational exchanges, but none as significant as the December meeting of the Iranian–Soviet standing commission. The Iraqis apparently realized that although Moscow renewed arms sales to them, the Kremlin was continuing to court the Khomeini regime and persisting in its game of playing both sides.[30] Iran, for its part, seemed to want to reemphasize to Moscow that Teheran was the more valuable Gulf partner and to tantalize the Kremlin with greater economic deals, should Moscow decide to end its support for Iraq.

For the USSR, 1987 presented the same problems as 1986. The continuation of the war created persistent problems in Soviet relations with the combatants and in Moscow's relations with the rest of the Muslim world (see next chapter). At the same time, the US seemed as determined as ever to play a major role in the region and offered to guarantee shipping throughout the region. Thus, the Soviets played the same careful balancing game; this time, however, there was a decided tilt toward Iraq despite high level Soviet–Iranian meetings.

In August 1986, Saddam Hussein issued a call for a cease-fire, a return to the recognized international boundaries, and a pledge of mutual noninterference. These themes were echoed in a major Soviet pronouncement on the war as reported on January 9, 1987, in *Izvestiia*. The page one editorial called for an end to the war through negotiation. It acknowledged that both sides have legitimate interests, called for territorial integrity, and denounced implicitly Iran's determination to overthrow the Saddam Hussein regime.[31]

The Soviet move was welcomed by Baghdad and largely ignored, if not condemned, by Teheran. In fact, Iran claimed that the USSR was "treading the path taken by the United States."[32] A week later Shevardnadze received the Iraqi ambassador to Moscow with whom he had a "friendly" conversation.

The Soviet tilt toward Iraq was manifest in several Soviet statements issued in early 1987. In an interview with the Kuwaiti *Al Anba'*, Igor Yevechenko, the deputy chief of the department of Near Eastern countries of the Ministry of Foreign Affairs, stated categorically that the Kremlin would "continue its support for Iraq in accordance with the friendship and cooperation agreement between the two countries, an agreement that covers *military*, economic, and cultural fields."[33]

As in the past, neither the escalation of the fighting—a renewed Iranian offensive toward Basra—nor the shift to a more overtly pro-Iraqi policy prevented the continuation of high level Soviet–Iranian contacts. In mid-February, Iranian foreign minister 'Ali Akbar Veleyati travelled to Moscow where he met with Eduard Shevardnadze, Andrei Gromyko, and Nikolai Ryzhkov. It is clear from both Soviet and Iranian coverage that the talks were less than successful. *Izvestiia* and TASS characterized the talks as a "frank, businesslike exchange of opinions." Despite the fact that Ryzhkov and Velayati agreed that the differences between the political systems should not prevent economic cooperation, Gromyko emphasized that the Kremlin would continue to condemn the Iranian position on the Iran–Iraq War. The Soviet president stated: "Our evaluation of this war and your views on it do not agree. . . . We believe that a more sensible soluion must be sought—in other words, ways to end this war."[34] Although this might seem like relatively mild disagreement, the fact that it appeared in print is another manifestation of *glasnost'*. Aleksandr Bovin, in a television commentary during Velayati's trip, further blasted Teheran's policies. As he had previously, he labelled the Khomeini regime a "theocratic dictatorship" and he explained the continuation of the war as a convenient way for Teheran to "write off" the difficulties of social development.[35]

In contrast to the Soviet version of the talks, the Iranian press painted a more positive picture. Velayati told the Teheran domestic service that positive and constructive understandings were reached. He added that the outcome of the visit would be seen in the near future. Furthermore, he indicated that Shevardnadze had accepted an invitation to visit Teheran. Most interestingly, Velayati said in the interview: "During our talks with the Soviet officials, we reminded them that the facilities they have provided the Iraqi regime are used to cause bloodshed in towns, to bomb populated areas, and to commit serious war crimes."[36] Velayati, in addition, rejected Western press reports which indicated that his trip had ended in failure.

The actual extent of disagreement between Velayati and the Soviets with whom he met was detailed in the Kuwaiti press. *Al Ra'y Al 'Amm* claimed that Moscow, in agreeing to Velayati's trip, responded to an urgent plea from Teheran. Reportedly, Velayati went to the USSR to urge the Kremlin to cease its supply of weapons to Baghdad and to pressure Saddam Hussein to end the bombing of Iranian cities.

> The sources said the Soviets rejected the Iranian minister's request and told him they were prepared to suspend arms supplies to Iraq and to pressure it to stop bombing Iranian cities if Iran responds to peace initiatives, ends the war, and issues an official communique in that regard.

Not only did Velayati reject this proposal, but he also threatened that Iran would turn "openly" toward the US if the bombardment did not cease. The article went on to allege that Moscow too had issued threats, specifically that its unhappiness with the Iran arms deal would lead the Kremlin to "take a different stand on the war."[37]

February and March brought renewed offensives in the area surrounding Basra. This was almost a replay of the year earlier when Kornienko travelled to Teheran and then Iran launched the Fao offensive. In the face of the Iranian attacks and undoubted Iraqi concern about the high level Soviet–Iranian meetings, Tariq Aziz went to the USSR within two weeks of the Velayati visit. The Soviet characterization of the atmospherics of the meeting indicate that there were both agreements and differences of opinion. TASS reported a "businesslike, substantive exchange of opinion."[38] Andrei Gromyko put a more positive gloss on the talks. Emphasizing the "friendly" nature of the ties, he said that "the Soviet Union further intends for its part to maintain these relations and contribute to their enrichment."[39]

The increasing complexity of the balancing game and the growing volatility of the war pushed the Soviet Union to shift its focus, for several months, to diplomacy toward the rest of the Gulf. In April 1987, the Kremlin dispatched Vladimir Petrovskii, a deputy foreign minister, to tour the Gulf. He was the highest ranking Soviet official to visit Oman and the UAE to date. The diplomatic trend was accelerated by Kuwait's request to both superpowers to protect its shipping. As will be discussed in the next chapter, the US and the USSR responded positively to the Kuwaiti appeal.

If events in the region impelled the Soviets to concentrate on diplomacy, then Gorbachev added his personal stamp by pursuing simultaneously a Soviet-sponsored mediation effort and a resolution to the conflict under UN auspices. In both cases, diplomacy was the key word and perhaps this is the new regime's strength. Gorbachev has brought *glasnost'* and polish to Soviet diplomacy. The newly reorganized Information Department of the Soviet Foreign Ministry, under the direction of Gennady Gerasimov, holds regular press briefings and the statements themselves are more interesting and agile. On the road, Soviet representatives are more accessible and apparently successful at presenting their cases.

In the final analysis, events in the war and in Gulf regional politics dictated, and will continue to dictate, Soviet policy options. With the prolongation of the war came new and increasingly dangerous problems for Soviet foreign policy decision-makers. The new initiatives—to be discussed in the chapters which follow—manifest an adeptness not previously seen in Moscow's foreign policy. Yet, that polish will be directed to responding to Gulf politics and to protecting traditional Soviet interests in the region.

Notes

1. *Pravda,* March 31, 1985, p. 4.

2. Moscow in Arabic, April 9, 1985, *FBIS SOV* 85 071, April 12, 1985, p. H4.

3. Yuri Glukhov, "Iran–Iraq: Exacerbation of Conflict," *Pravda,* March 20, 1985, p. 5.

4. Herbert H. Denton, "Iraq's Apparent Goading of Iran Nearly Backfired," *Washington Post,* March 25, 1985, pp. A1, A6.

5. V. Pustov, "Senseless and Dangerous Conflict," *Krasnaia zvezda,* March 24, 1985, p. 3.

6. KUNA, April 5, 1985, *FBIS SOV* 85 067, April 8, 1985, p. H1.

7. TASS, July 3, 1985, *FBIS SOV* 85 129, July 5, 1985, p. H1.

8. Richard Harwood and Don Oberdorfer, "China Now Largest Supplier of Arms to Iran, U.S. Says," *Washington Post,* August 26, 1986, pp. 1, 14.

9. "International Panorama," August 25, 1985, *FBIS SOV* 85 165, August 26, 1985, p. H3.

10. Tokyo, August 12, 1985, *FBIS SOV* 85 156, August 13, 1985, p. H7.

11. Moscow to Iran, September 9, 1985, *FBIS SOV* 85 176, September 11, 1985, p. H2.

12. Report dated December 11, 1985, pp. 1, 16, *Foreign Broadcast Information Service, Middle East and North Africa,* (hereafter *FBIS MEA*) 85 240, December 13, 1985, pp. E1-2.

13. TASS, December 16, 1985, *FBIS SOV* 85 242, December 17, 1985, p. H2.

14. *Pravda,* December 18, 1985, p. 4, *FBIS SOV* 85 243, December 18, 1985, p. H3.

15. Baghdad, Voice of the Masses, December 17, 1985, *FBIS SOV* 85 244, December 19, 1985, p. H1, 2.

16. *Pravda,* December 18, 1985, p. 4, *FBIS SOV* 85 243, December 18, 1985, p. H5.

17. First report *al Thawrah;* second *al Jumhuriah, FBIS MEA* 85 243, December 18, 1985, p. E1.

18. *Jordan Times,* December 23, 1985, pp. 1, 2 in *FBIS MEA* 85 246, December 23, 1985, pp. E2, 3.

19. See for example: QNA report December 19, 1985, in *FBIS SOV* 85 244, December 19, 1985, p. H2.

20. V. Komarov, *New Times,* No. 3, January 27, 1986, pp. 29-30.

21. *Middle East Economic Digest,* March 15, 1986, p. 18.

22. TASS, March 19, 1986, *FBIS SOV* March 20, 1986, p. H1.

23. *Al Hawadith,* in Arabic, March 28, 1986, pp. 35-37, in *FBIS SOV* 86 063, April 2, 1986, pp. H1-8.

24. TASS, April 19, 1986, *FBIS SOV* 86 076, April 21, 1986, p. H6.

25. Moscow TV, June 13, 1986, *FBIS SOV* 86 115, June 16, 1986, p. H1.

26. *The Boston Globe,* August 26, 1986, p. 10.

27. *The Wall Street Journal,* August 26, 1986, p. 29.

28. Igor Belaiev, "Iranian Gambit," *Literaturnaia gazeta,* November 26, 1986, p. 9.

29. Gorbachev speech to Indian Parliament, November 27, 1986, in *FBIS SOV* 86 229, November 28, 1986, pp. D6-12.

30. Interview with senior Iraqi officials, December, 1986.

31. *Izvestiia,* January 9, 1987, p. 1.

32. *FBIS MEA* 87 007, January 12, 1987, p. i.

33. *Al Anba',* January 13, 1987, pp. 1, 26, in *FBIS SOV* 87 013, January 21, 1987, pp. H1-2. Emphasis added.

34. *Izvestiia,* February 15, 1987, p. 1.

35. Moscow TV, February 15, 1987, in *FBIS SOV* 87 033, February 19, 1987, pp. H5-6.

36. Teheran Domestic Service, February 14, 1987, *FBIS MEA* 87 032, February 18, 1987, p. I4.

37. Kuwait, *Al Ra'y Al 'Amm,* February 15, 1987, pp. 1, 18 in *FBIS SOV* 87 036, February 24, 1987, pp. H5-6.

38. TASS, February 20, 1987, *FBIS SOV* 87 034, February 20, 1987, p. H1.

39. *Izvestiia,* February 22, 1987, p. 1, 4.

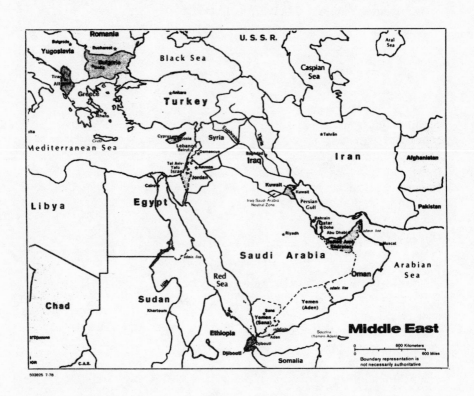

4

The Diplomatic Offensive

Since the outbreak of the Gulf War, the Soviets have not only been
concerned wih equalizing their links to Iran and Iraq, but also have
had to contend with the fallout from the war in the Arab world. As
the war continued, it became increasingly clear to all that other Middle
East issues and actors could not long remain isolated from the Gulf
War. Indeed, the conflict has driven home the lesson that events in the
Gulf bear directly on other Middle East issues central to the Kremlin's
concerns. The war exacerbated preexisting fissure among the Arabs, in
some cases hardening antipathies between Soviet clients. Moreover, the
prolonged war also facilitated a rebirth of regionalism in the form of
the Gulf Cooperation Council. (For the Soviets, regionalism is a positive
force only so long as it is anti-Western.) Finally, the Iran–Iraq War
also set in motion a significant shift in the pattern of Arab alliances.
Each of these developments deflected attention from the Arab–Israeli
dispute and complicated Soviet Middle East strategies designed to
promote a unified anti-Israel, anti-American, position. The new regional
environment created by the war dictated that long-term Soviet strategies
in the Middle East needed to be amended. Kremlin political strategists,
therefore, had to decide which policy options the USSR should pursue
to contain the negative ramifications of the war.

Arab Alliances

The engine driving Soviet involvement in the Middle East has been
the Arab–Israeli dispute. Despite Soviet support for the partition of
Palestine and although Moscow provided arms to Israel in the forties,
by 1956 the USSR had clearly chosen the Arab side in the on-going
conflict. Since then, the USSR has pursued a policy designed to promote
Arab unity, and the logical basis for that unity is hostility to Israel.
Soviet propaganda beamed at the Middle East consistently emphasizes
that the major issue in the region is Israeli occupation of lands captured

in 1967 and that any rivalries, political disputes, or border conflicts are detrimental to the goal of rallying all forces against Israel. This thrust is designed to preclude tough decisions, and to promote anti-Americanism.

Consistent with its policy of bolstering Arab unity, the Soviet leadership reacted cautiously to all major flare-ups of Arab rivalries. For example, in 1977 when tensions between Libya and Egypt erupted into a four-day border war, Moscow called for an immediate cease-fire. Even though Egyptian president Anwar Sadat was clearly reorienting Egyptian policy at the time, the USSR claimed that the rift between Muammar Qaddafi and Sadat was diverting attention from the Arab cause. The Soviets, too, urged a peaceful solution to the conflict between Morocco and Algeria over the Western Sahara. They wanted to avoid a choice because of their long-standing economic interest in the Kingdom of Morocco and close long-lived political ties to Algeria. Moscow has also tried to mediate the long-standing rivalry between the Iraqi and Syrian wings of the Ba'ath Party. This antagonism has caused Moscow nothing but headaches since, in this case, two radicals—both Soviet clients—face off with propaganda attacks and alleged incidents of sabotage. Despite a short-lived reconciliation in the fall of 1978 and spring of 1979, the enmity continues unabated.

The rules of Middle East politics remained fairly constant until Egyptian president Anwar Sadat's historic trip to Jerusalem in November 1977. His journey altered the axioms of regional politics and created a series of alignments in the Middle East that endured until at least the outbreak of the Gulf War. At one end of the spectrum were the so-called conservative states of Egypt, Oman, and Somalia, which backed the Egyptian–Israeli peace treaty and by extension supported US mediation efforts. At the other extreme were the "rejectionists," Syria, Libya, the People's Democratic Republic of Yemen (PDRY), the PLO, Algeria, and initially Iraq. Between these two poles lay the majority of the Arab states which, while condemning Camp David, were comparatively pro-Western and not nearly as "radical" as the rejectionists. In this period between the initiation of the "Camp David Process," and the Iraqi attack on Iran, the USSR worked not only to cultivate opposition to the peace agreements, but also to move the moderates closer to the radical camp. At the very least, hostility to Israel could provide Moscow with common viewpoints even among the so-called moderates and conservatives.

The initiation of hostilities on September 22 disrupted this pattern. With the outbreak of open warfare, Syria moved immediately to support Iran. The brief romance between Baghdad and Damascus had cooled when Saddam Hussein assumed power in the summer of 1979. By

March 1980, the two reverted to their prior hostile stands and in August, the Hussein regime claimed that Syria was plotting to overthrow the Baghdad government. From the Soviet perspective, it was not that the war cut short the rapprochement, but that the outbreak of hostilities finalized the break. If Moscow held any expectations of Arab unity even among the radicals, then Syrian backing for Teheran shattered those hopes. Other Middle East actors also chose sides in the Gulf War. In addition to Syria, Libya opted to back Iran. As noted in Chapter 2, Libya has transshipped Soviet military equipment to Teheran since the conflict began. Algeria and the Peoples' Democratic Republic of Yemen also espoused the Iranian cause, although less enthusiastically than Syria or Libya.

On the Iraqi side of the scorecard were Jordan, the Sudan, and Oman. The traditional Middle East addage, my enemy's enemy is my friend, seemingly prevailed. The hostility between Amman and Damascus over Palestinian issues undoubtedly helped put King Hussein squarely in Baghdad's camp. Within a month of the outbreak of the war, the king had flown to Baghdad to express his support for Saddam Hussein. In the case of the Sudan, President Numeiri's dislike of Qaddafi prompted the staunchly pro-Iraqi position. These states were joined by the Yemen Arab Republic (YAR), Morocco, Tunisia, Oman, and Egypt. Morocco and Tunisia were impelled at least in part by Maghrebi concerns, namely Qaddafi's support of the POLISARIO and his backing of anti-government rebels in Tunisia. The Egyptian case is unique among these. Egypt, in an action which elicited unbridled hostility from the Khomeini regime, permitted the Shah residence until his death. Following Sadat's assassination by Islamic fundamentalists, his successor, Hosni Mubarak, toned down some of Sadat's rhetoric, while continuing to support Iraq.

For the Soviet Union, the definition of the pro-Iraqi and pro-Iranian camps meant that potential clients wound up on opposing sides. In some cases, the USSR had long histories of involvement with these states. Indeed, looking at the list one notes that the Soviet Union has signed friendship and cooperation treaties with states on both sides. It has a treaty with Syria and the PDRY on one side; and on the pro-Iraqi side, has a treaty with Iraq, of course, and in 1984 signed one with the YAR. Although the issues separating several of these states predate the outbreak of the Iran–Iraq War, the choice of sides certainly added to the list of grievances. Moscow, therefore, had to be additionally careful of conflict between clients.

The war also affected intraregional alliances on the Arabian Peninsula. With a push from Saudi Arabia, the Gulf states moved to create the Gulf Cooperation Council. The GCC held its first meeting in May

1981. Initially a purely economic and political organization, the GCC has grown to include military and security ties among its members. The states are instinctively pro-Iraqi, but their proximity to Iran had led them to temper some of their support for Baghdad. In general, Moscow has adopted careful approaches to regional organizations— approaches which vary by region and by issue. Where regional organizations seek to exclude *all* foreign influences, the Soviets have been exceptionally wary. From the Kremlin's perspective, the GCC was a pro-American organization primarily because Saudi Arabia, a major US client, was its prime mover, and secondarily because Oman agreed to US bases and has carried out joint maneuvers with American forces.

The war has probably had the greatest impact on alliance patterns because it blurred the lines among the traditional Arab groupings. In the late seventies, Iraq was isolated both in the Gulf and in the Middle East as a whole. As noted in Chapter 2, in the summer preceeding the war, Saddam Hussein launched a major diplomatic initiative to garner support for the impending conflict. As a result, after September 1980, the Iraqis moved to make their peace with Saudi Arabia. In December 1981, the two settled their outstanding border conflict and in spring 1982 the Iraqi vice president met with King Khalid. On January 18, 1983, Saddam Hussein travelled to Riyadh to further the rapprochement. Concomitantly, Iraq tempered its "rejectionist" stands. As a counter to the apparent Soviet tilt toward Teheran in the first two years of the war, the Baghdad government sent signals that it was willing to ameliorate ties with Washington. During the August 1982 visit of Representative Stephen Solarz to Baghdad, Saddam Hussein indicated that Iraq was perhaps rethinking its position on the Arab– Israeli dispute. In part, Iraqi policy has been dictated by hostile relations with Assad's Syria. Making every effort to stymie Syrian policy with regard to Israel, the Iraqis have, at the same time, had to be careful not to appear to sanction separate deals with Tel Aviv.[1]

Saddam's coalition building strategy, coupled with his search for military support, opened the doors for Cairo's reintegration into the Arab fold. Growing out of military necessity—the Egyptians possess large stockpiles of surplus Soviet military equipment—Saddam Hussein softened his condemnation of Egypt and of the peace treaty. In December 1982, the Iraqi president announced that Iraq "looked forward to Egypt's resumption of its natural role in the pan-Arab environment."[2] This statement came days after an Iraqi military delegation concluded talks on Iraqi-Egyptian military cooperation. In early January 1983, Egyptian foreign minister Butros Butros Ghali met with Tariq Aziz in Paris, initiating diplomatic contacts as well. Between January and July, an agreement was reached whereby Egypt would sell Iraq Soviet-made weapons. And then in August 1983, the first official Egyptian ministerial delegation travelled to Baghdad. In December 1983, Butros Ghali announced that 1984 would bring "far reaching developments" in relations between Cairo and Baghdad. In March 1986, President Hosni Mubarak visited Baghdad with King Hussein of Jordan and diplomatic relations were reestablished in November 1987.

As part of the movement toward the new Arab configuration, ties between Amman and Cairo improved as well. By the end of 1983, the two Arab states resumed trade, and in early 1984, King Hussein called for Egypt's readmission to the Arab League. The King clearly had decided that the tense situation in the Arab world (over the Gulf War and Palestinian issues) made it far less dangerous than previously to deal with the Egyptians. 1984 proved a decisive year for Egypt. On January 7, Saudi prince Talal bin Abd al Aziz visited Egypt. The trip was the first by a member of the royal family since 1977. Also in January, the Islamic Conference Organization formally readmitted Egypt. It should be noted that Syria, Libya, and the PDRY walked out in protest. By the fall of 1984, Jordan and Egypt restored full diplomatic relations and in January 1985, it was reported that the two signed a strategic cooperation agreement. Moscow thus had to contend with a much reinforced moderate camp.

This in turn diminished the strength of radical Arab councils, leaving Syria and Libya on the periphery. Syrian support for Iran and Jordanian backing of Iraq led to heightened tensions on the Jordanian–Syrian border. Moreover, Assad's choice of sides lessened Arab support for Syria when Israel annexed the Golan Heights in 1981. Well aware of mounting Syrian isolation, President Assad travelled to the Gulf to explain the Syrian position. Yet, when faced with a major crisis in the Israeli invasion of Lebanon, Syria received only tepid support from the Arab world. The response was far less than what might have been expected earlier. Again, in 1983, when the US attacked Syria in retaliation for Syrian firing on US reconnaissance planes, moderate Arabs did not rally to Damascus's side. Libya, Iran's other staunch supporter, remains isolated as well. Of course, Qaddafi's isolation is as much a product of his adventurist African policies and his penchant for trouble-making as it is of his support of Teheran. Yet, the latter clearly magnified the distrust already existing. Beginning almost immediately after the start of the war, Qaddafi proclaimed it each state's Islamic duty to back Iran in the war. This move upset several of the Arab countries, including Saudi Arabia which alleged that Qaddafi was distorting the Islamic cause. And in October 1980, Saudi Arabia severed diplomatic relations with Tripoli.

In a move which further complicated intra-Arab politics, Libya invited Teheran to attend a meeting of the so-called rejectionist front which convened in Benghazi in September 1981. Although Teheran is ardently rejectionist, its presence within the front proved counterproductive to the cause. Because of Iran's presence, the final communique made no mention of the Gulf War which was by then a pressing issue on the Arab agenda. Moreover, "radicals" such as Algeria objected to the organization's attenuation of ties with the Arab world.[3] If anything, the insertion of Iran into the Arab forum deflected attention from the Arab–Israeli arena and from the Palestinians. The addition of Iran to the rejectionist camp hastened its demise. Strife within the front prevented it from taking an active role during the 1982 Lebanese war. Indeed by January 1983, the front had been diminished by the absence of Algeria, the PDRY, and the PLO. While they declined to attend a meeting held in Damascus, Iran, Syria, and Libya called for the overthrow of Saddam Hussein. Presently, the front is, for all practical purposes, dead. As a result of these changes, many Arab states resent the intrusion of non-Arab Iran into Arab politics because it was Khomeini's rhetoric directed toward Baghdad which helped to precipitate the Gulf War. Moreover, Qaddafi and Assad bear indirect responsibility for the Iranian factor.

What has this done to Soviet stakes and ambitions in the Middle East? In the first instance, Moscow's relations with Syria and with Libya have never been easy. Each bilateral tie is laden with problems as each state pursues its own objectives—sometimes contrary to the USSR's—in the region. While much has been written elsewhere on the Kremlin's troubled alliances with Assad and Qaddafi,[4] it is important to note here that each one's ties with Iran proved to be both a plus and a minus to the Soviets. When each shipped Soviet equipment to Teheran, it provided Moscow with an indirect means to maintain and to cultivate relations with the new Islamic government in Iran. Yet, as the war has become a major foreign policy dilemma to the Soviet leadership, both Assad and Qaddafi have been pressured to lessen their support, or at least to declare their neutrality in the conflict. In the wider Middle East context, the isolation of Syria and Libya, which certainly is underscored by their backing of Teheran, limits Soviet maneuverability. It ill serves Soviet purposes to have its sole remaining confrontationist client, Syria, isolated in the region. In the Libyan case, the Kremlin leadership has to deal with a host of issues, including Iran, which forces them to keep Qaddafi at arm's length. In the early 1980s, therefore, Moscow's Middle East fortunes had definitely worsened. Events had overtaken objectives and strategies. When Iraq attacked Iran in September 1980, opposition to the Israeli-Egyptian peace treaty was still an overriding political concern. As long as Egypt was the pariah of the Arab world, Moscow's task to promote oppositon to the US-brokered Camp David Accords was easy. If Soviet goals were to use anti-Israel feelings and by extension the ostracism of Egypt, then the war proved extremely detrimental to Soviet policy objectives. Once Cairo has been even partially readmitted into the fold, resistance to any US role was thereby lessened. It became more difficult for Moscow to promote its well-worn slogans of anti-Americanism and anti-Israeli positions.

It is of course an oversimplification to say that the Iran–Iraq War alone was the cause of the new divisions in the Arab world. Questions relating to the Israeli invasion of Lebanon and to the Syrian attack on the Arafat wing of the PLO certainly play a major role. Nonetheless, the new alignments prevented Arab League meetings; prevented decisions from being taken when they did convene; and prevented any kind of decisive joint action with regard to the Palestinian dilemma or Lebanon. The Arab coalition was in disarray, "rejectionism" was fading, and close Soviet clients were regarded warily by the fellow Arabs. There seemed to be tacit recognition that a US role was a necessity in the Arab-Israeli arena. Thus, Soviet decision-makers needed to craft a policy which could better their fortunes.

Active Diplomacy

Until 1985, the only Gulf state with which the Soviets maintained relations was Kuwait. Common ground between the two could be found in both Kuwait's opposition to foreign involvement in the region and its support of the Palestinians and the Arab cause. During official visits, the Soviet press characterized relations as "friendly" and praised Kuwait for its independence. In 1974 and 1976, the Kuwaitis concluded arms agreements with Moscow, including weapons sales, military training assistance, and the construction of a port and an air base. Again in 1980, the two countries negotiated an arms deal reported to be worth $200 million. The contract included SA6 and SA7 as well as FROG 7 missiles.[5]

Following the outbreak of the Gulf War, Kuwait sought closer Soviet ties. In April 1981, Sheikh Sabah, the Kuwaiti foreign minister, travelled to Moscow. During the visit, he seconded Soviet calls for an international conference on the Middle East and reiterated Moscow's statements that the Indian Ocean be converted into a "zone of peace."[6] Nonetheless, these wide areas of agreement could not mask serious Kuwaiti opposition to the invasion and occupation of Afghanistan. Again in the spring of 1984, when the tanker war began, the Kuwaitis sought international protection from both superpowers. In May, Sheikh Sabah appealed to Washington to sell Kuwait stinger missiles. Congressional opposition prevented the sale, but the Pentagon prepared a series of options to help bolster Kuwaiti air defenses.[7] In the wake of the US refusal, Kuwait's defense minister travelled to Moscow. The Soviet coverage of the visit stressed long-standing good relations between the two and their agreement on some of the crucial Middle East and Persian Gulf questions. Moscow, underscoring Kuwait's opposition to foreign bases in the region, clearly tried to put Kuwait's membership in the Gulf Cooperation Council in the best light. KUNA revealed that, according to Sheikh Salim as-Sabah, Dmitri Ustinov "confirmed" that the USSR would be "happy to satisfy all Kuwait's needs for various weapons."[8] At the time of the visit, Moscow agreed to sell Kuwait surface-to-air and surface-to-surface missiles. Estimates of the price tag ran from $200–$300 million.[9] As is the common practice, the arms deal was not announced in the Soviet press. Reportedly the deal included the stationing of Soviet military personnel in Kuwait to assist in training Kuwaiti soldiers on the new equipment. Despite the size and scope of this new deal, the Kuwaitis denied that it constituted a military treaty. According to KUNA, the Sheikh stated categorically that the agreement did "not concern bases or other facilities. . . ."[10]

The Kuwaiti arms deal was evidently designed to show that Moscow could help the Gulf Arabs more than Washington. The accord came as the USSR began a campaign to improve its position in the Middle East and to ameliorate ties with the Gulf states. If nothing else, the Soviet leadership hoped that Kuwait could be an example for other Gulf states to follow.

Prized among the Gulf states, of course, would be Saudi Arabia. From the Soviet perspective, Saudi Arabia is an American client and a major conservative force in the Middle East. More than once in the sixties and seventies, Moscow and Riyadh found themselves on opposing sides of local conflicts. During the civil war in North Yemen, the Kremlin aided republican forces, while the Saudis backed the royalists. Details of the civil war period are beyond the scope of this work. Nonetheless, it should be noted that Soviet support for the eventually victorious republicans included the supply of military equipment and the presence of Soviet pilots who flew air cover for the republican troops. Moscow also provided military and political assistance to the Popular Front for the Liberation of Oman which sought to overthrow the Sultan of Oman. Despite Soviet intervention, Sultan Qabus was able to mitigate the threat to his regime with Saudi and Iranian assistance. These differences notwithstanding, the Soviet leadership would not write off Riyadh. At the time of the US-brokered

Camp David Accords which Saudi Arabia opposed, Moscow appeared to try to use the tensions in the Saudi–US relationship. Several public statements at the time foresaw better Moscow–Riyadh ties. Yet, whatever slim hope there might have been was short-lived and dashed by the invasion of Afghanistan. According to the Saudis, the continuing occupation of Afghanistan was an obstacle to any significant changes in Soviet–Saudi relations.

The Saudi monarchy, of course, is not without its difficulties. There have been workers' strikes and other political disturbances. Although some of these groups received positive Soviet media coverage, Moscow has not offered any real support. Basically, the Kremlin leadership does not appear to be terribly sanguine about their prospects. Soviet pessimism notwithstanding, at the time of the Iranian revolution, Soviet observers foresaw a similar pattern emerging in other conservative monarchies including Saudi Arabia. As one writer put it:

> The people's revolution in Iran which ended the pro-American despotic regime left the Saudi monarchy pondering . . . how dangerous [was] the unlimited support of the United States.
>
> The fate of the Shah showed that rapid economic development heated up by the "oil boom" in conditions of the preservation of traditional social and political structures not only doesn't resolve socio-economic, political and ideological problems of a developing society, but indeed can sharpen them to a scale dangerous for the political regime. . . .[11]

These themes are both a warning to the monarchy not to depend solely on the US and, in a sense, an advertisement that Moscow was waiting in the wings.

By 1982, when the consequences of the Iranian revolution became clear to Moscow observers, they returned to more conventional approaches. Despite the obvious conservatism of the Saudi monarchy, and despite the potential for economic and social dislocations, the Soviets are clearly desirous of establishing diplomatic relations. In December 1982, an Arab League delegation that included the Saudi foreign minister visited Moscow. Seizing the opportunity, Soviet propaganda mills ground out commentaries urging the regularization of ties despite differing social systems. For their part, the Saudis announced that Riyadh was considering various forms of cooperation with the Soviet Union.

What they seemed to be considering was increased trade. Although the Saudis have traditionally purchased some industrial goods from the USSR, beginning in 1983, the Kingdom began to sell fuel and raw materials to Moscow. The Soviets imported approximately 156 million rubles worth of products, while they exported only 12.9 million rubles.[12] The imbalance continues at about the same level.

In 1984, as they had briefly in 1978–1979, the Soviets sought to improve ties with Saudi Arabia. In the spring, a major dispute erupted over congressional opposition to the sale of Stinger missiles to Riyadh. So as to signal its displeasure, the monarchy hinted to the Russians that an amelioration of relations might be in the offing. In fact, Soviet ambassador Anatoly Dobrynin was invited to dine at the Saudi embassy in Washington, D.C.[13] This opening, too, was short-lived. Events in the Gulf War—an Iranian attack on a Saudi tanker and the Saudi downing of an Iranian jet—sped up the rapprochement between Washington and Riyadh. Despite this on-again, off-again flirtation, the Soviets saw fit to continue to push for better ties. They praised whatever low-level contacts there were and sought to use Saudi Arabia's hostility to Israel to further relations.

In the interregnum between Brezhnev's death and Gorbachev's accession to power, the other significant event was the signing of a friendship and cooperation treaty between Moscow and Sanaa. As previously noted, the USSR had long-standing ties to the YAR which date back to the 1950s. Military assistance flowed to the Imam as early as 1958, but when the Imam was overthrown, the Kremlin sided with the republican forces. Following their victory, ties remained friendly, but not so close as to preclude relations with the United States or even US military aid.

The Soviet relationship with Sanaa has been complicated over the years by Moscow's ties to the PDRY. Although the Soviet–PDRY connection has been rocky at times, things improved considerably in the mid- to late-seventies. Several economic and military agreements were concluded and Aden played host to Cuban and East German advisors. In 1979, following a bizarre series of events, the Kremlin and the PDRY signed a friendship and cooperation treaty. It seems that by the late seventies, then president Rubai Ali, feeling hemmed in by the strong Soviet and Cuban presence in his country, maneuvered to assert the PDRY's independence: Among other strategies, he strengthened Aden's ties both to Saudi Arabia and to the YAR. On June 24, 1978, the president of North Yemen was assassinated allegedly by agents of the PDRY. The pro-Soviet elements within the PDRY leadership charged Ali's complicity, and seized power with the help of Cuban troops stationed in Aden. Two days later Ali and several of his closest associates were executed. The new pro-Soviet leader Abdul Fattah Ismail proclaimed Marxism–Leninism in Yemen and created the Yemen Socialist Party. Following his assumption of power, the PDRY attacked the north—a move that did not sit well with either Moscow or the

Arab world. Under Arab League sponsorship, a cease-fire was declared in March 1979 and the two Yemens began negotiations to merge. Less than a year later, in December, the friendship treaty with Moscow was initialed.

Given the tribal problems in the region and periodic border wars, the Soviets have been able to play a very careful balancing game. The tightrope walk can be seen in the very fact of the signing of the 1984 treaty with YAR and in its language. A careful reading of the treaty text reveals both some similarities and some differences from the agreement with the PDRY. As with all the friendship and cooperation treaties, the first several articles of the YAR treaty deal with issues—such as the Middle East question, anti-imperialism, and anti-Zionism—on which there is agreement. The treaty also contains a clause similar to other treaties calling for "mutual consultations" regarding "international problems which affect both countries' interests." Moreover, article 7 provides that neither will participate in actions directed against the other.[14] In sharp contrast, the treaty with South Yemen implies a much closer relationship: In addition to the clauses on mutual consultations and furthering cooperation, the PDRY treaty includes three distinctive clauses. First, article 5 deals directly with military cooperation "in the interests of strengthening their defensive capabilities." Second, article 10 specifically mentions agreement on Soviet proposals to create a "security system" and demilitarized zone in the Indian Ocean. Finally, article 12 spells out that neither will participate in military or other alliances directed against the other.[15]

For Moscow, the treaty represented a short term success in preventing either the US or Saudi Arabia from establishing a predominent influence position. Yet, in the longer run, the history of border wars between the two Yemens and their support to opposing forces in the Gulf War presents the possibility of future conflict. Moscow has thus far avoided having to chose between the two; but Chernenko made it clear at the reception for North Yemen's president that he was well aware of a potential problem. He stressed, more than once, that the treaty with the YAR was not directed against any third country—namely the PDRY.

I would like to make the following point in this connection. During the past week, we have had good and frank conversations with the leaders of the two Yemen states, the People's Democratic Republic of Yemen and the Yemen Arab Republic. We are sincerely gladdened by the spirit of mutual respect and good-neighborliness that characterizes relations between those two Arab states.[16]

Merger possibilities have been discussed and the Soviets, as they had on the Horn of Africa, enthusiastically endorsed the proposals. However, ideological differences and historic antipathies would seem to preclude the idea.

Gorbachev and Gulf Diplomacy

Thus, by the time Mikhail Gorbachev became general secretary, Soviet fortunes had improved somewhat in the Gulf. Not only had Moscow formalized its link to the YAR, but it had also reemphasized its readiness to aid Kuwait and by extension other Arab states when the US proved unwilling. At the same time, the USSR's problems in the Arab–Israeli arena continued. As long as Israel remained in southern Lebanon, the potential for a Syrian–Israeli confrontation loomed large and dangerous. In the wake of the US debacle in Lebanon, Moscow moved to shore up its alliance with Hafiz al Assad. The Israeli withdrawal reduced the possibility of the two clients dragging their superpower patrons into a war, but did not alleviate the communal conflict in Lebanon which involved Soviet client Syria. The Kremlin also proposed a new Middle East peace plan devised to garner Arab—even moderate Arab—support.

Given the Arab–Israeli situation as it existed in 1985, the new Soviet leadership sent clear signals that change was required. Although President Assad's standing was to improve when he effected the release of the hostages from a TWA flight hijacked to Beirut, he remained on the periphery of the Arab world. In July, the Soviet ambassador to France met with the Israeli ambassador in Paris. It was rumored at the time that Moscow was interested in renewing diplomatic relations with Tel Aviv. This made perfect sense for the Kremlin which feared being excluded from yet another US-brokered peace agreement. Soviet fortunes were to improve still further in the wake of the *Achille Lauro* hijacking. It will be recalled that the US forced down an Egyptian jet carrying the hijackers. The resulting strain in US–Egyptian relations was one from which Moscow hoped to benefit.

Moscow thus showed increasing flexibility toward the Middle East in 1985 and its diplomatic initiatives were to pay off in the Gulf as well. Changes did occur in 1985 when Oman and the United Arab Emirates (UAE) established diplomatic relations with Moscow for the first time. Oman and the USSR broke the ice in September 1985, when Shevardnadze met his Omani counterpart during that year's UN General Assembly meeting. The official communique announcing the opening of ties emphasized mutual respect and noninterference. It also claimed that the establishment of relations "meets the interests of both countries."[17] Soviet commentary on the move presented it as a logical occurrence because of Moscow's support of Arab causes. *Pravda* noted as well that the war impelled the Sultan to "diversify methods of safeguarding [Oman's] security."[18] According to Omani media, the establishment of diplomtic relations resulted from two years of contacts and was a response to the "new trend" in Soviet foreign policy under Gorbachev.[19] In all probability the Omanis were seeking additional protection from the Gulf War; but, Oman also intended the act as a slap on Washington's wrist. The previous spring as Oman and the US renegotiated a basing agreement, the Omanis reportedly were annoyed when details of the negotiations were released in the *New York Times*. The front page article portrayed Oman as an invaluable US asset, but described the Sultan in less than flattering terms.[20] Moscow was only too pleased to take advantage of the situation. Yet, while the Soviets may count their new ties to Oman as a success, Oman did not permit a resident Soviet ambassador.

That November, the UAE became the third GCC state to establish diplomatic links with the Kremlin. For the Emirates, as with Oman, the move was an insurance policy. It demonstrated the UAE's nonalignment which, it was hoped, would be a shield against Iranian attack. The Emirates too apparently felt that with the new Soviet leader in the Kremlin, the timing was propitious for the change. For the Soviets, the establishment of formal ties meant another breakthrough in a region where hitherto they had been excluded.

With the addition of Oman and the UAE to the list of GCC states with relations with Moscow, the Soviets revised their estimation of the council. No longer an imperialist tool, the GCC was seen now as a neutral organization which opposed foreign interference. In November 1985, *Krasnaia zvezda* stressed the GCC's role in countering the US and Israeli threat to the area. "Along with the adoption of a specific program of collective actions to ensure security and defense, the leaders of the GCC pointed to the necessity to expand sources of arms in the 'national interest of the council countries.'"[21]

The change in tone in Soviet pronouncements may be seen as part of Gorbachev's new sophisticated and dexterous cultivation effort. Nonetheless, the GCC still tended to view the USSR warily. In an interesting interview, the secretary general of the GCC, Ya'qub Bisharah, stressed that Moscow continued to misunderstand the GCC. The council pursues development and not change, while the Soviet Union "is not a state that stands for the status quo." Moreover, the USSR underestimates the desire of the Gulf states to maintain their independence. Moscow believes that the GCC can be influenced by the United States. In an insightful summary, Bisharah said: "The Soviet attitude toward the GCC will remain cautious and cool while Moscow will continue to seek to develop relations *bilaterally.*"[22]

The flush of relative successes of the fall of 1985 and of Gorbachev's first ten months in power faded in January 1986 when domestic turmoil in the PDRY seemed to jeopardize the Soviet standing on the peninsula. The PDRY, the sole Marxist–Leninist Arab state, has hosted a large number of Soviet military and civilian dignitaries. Additionally, although there are no Soviet bases, *per se,* Soviet air and naval forces enjoy almost unfettered access to the PDRY's facilities.[23] Aden provided airlift facilities during the fighting on the Horn of Africa and training facilities to PLO and PFLO guerrillas. But the politics of the regime of Ali Nasir Muhammad created dilemmas for Moscow. On the one hand, the PDRY's radicalism over the years alarmed its peninsula neighbors. On the other, when Ali tempered Aden's policies, Moscow grew concerned over the extent of that moderation. Thus in March 1985, the Kremlin permitted the previous leader, Abdul Fattah Ismail (who had been in exile in Moscow and who was considered a radical), to return to Aden. The hope was to persuade Ali to reradicalize his course, but not to the extent of threatening his neighbors. The plan clearly backfired: When factional fighting intensified, Ali attempted to assassinate his rivals at a Politburo meeting in mid-January.

The massacre at the Politburo unleashed a ten-day civil war that caught the Kremlin by surprise. The Soviets were at risk in several ways. A significant radicalization of the PDRY's foreign policy would alienate Aden's neighbors, particularly the YAR and Oman, and jeopardize the newly constructed ties. In fact, as the internal situation stabilized, Moscow tried to assure the peninsula states that Aden's foreign policy wouldn't change. By the same token, if Ali Nasir Muhammad had been victorious, he might well have blamed Moscow for the problems and moved to attenuate ties with the Kremlin.

From all indications, the USSR closely monitored the civil war. It was reported in the Gulf press that Moscow had established a watching post in Ethiopia. Furthermore, the PDRY prime minister, who happened to be in New Delhi at the time, flew on to Moscow where he waited out the storm and consulted with Soviet officials. At first, the Soviets stayed out of the fray; however, they ultimately decided to side with the pro-Ismail forces which proved victorious. A Soviet ship aided the rebels by boosting their radio broadcasts and it was reported that the Soviets provided small arms to the rebels.[24] According to the French ambassador to Aden, the Soviets unloaded a large number of crates in Aden claiming that they were medical supplies. Pierre Audebert added: "I doubt it."[25]

As it was, both the new government in the PDRY and the USSR sought to regularize relations as quickly as possible. By the end of January, the Gulf press reported an "urgent" Soviet resupply of the Yemeni armed forces. During this same period, Moscow sent medical teams and construction crews to the scene. There were also several meetings in Aden between various PDRY officials and the Soviet ambassador, Vladislav Zhukov. For their part, the victorious rebels convened an emergency politburo meeting at which Al 'Attas was appointed president. Moreover, the plenum reaffirmed the PDRY's "proletarian internationalism" and thanked the Soviet Union for its support. The PDRY delegation to the twenty-seventh CPSU congress met with Yegor Ligachev and Geidar Aliev for "friendly" conversations. According to TASS, they "reiterated the mutual striving of the CPSU and the Yemen Socialist Party for strengthening inter-party contacts and for expanding relations between the Soviet Union and Democratic Yemen on the basis of their treaty of friendship and cooperation."[26] In his speech to the congress, Ali Salim Al Bayd, the new general secretary, reaffirmed unity with his fellow rejectionists, Libya, Syria, and Algeria and thanked the Soviet Union for its "internationalist solidarity."[27] The intensified contacts continued at all levels: Al Bayd met with Gorbachev in Berlin in April and trade union and economic delegations met in both Aden and Moscow. In June, Prime Minister Nu'man travelled to Moscow for three days of consultations. He met with Ryzhkov for "friendly" talks, while Shevardnadze held discussions with the foreign minister. That July another Soviet delegation flew to Aden and in September the deputy foreign minister met with Politburo member Aliev in Moscow. Agreements were reached on agriculture and media exchanges.

Otherwise, the parade of Gulf state officials to Moscow and of Soviet dignitaries to the peninsula states continued as expected. As the accompanying charts indicate, the Soviet Union maintained its diplomatic effort well into 1986. The YAR, in particular, was the object of Soviet courtship in an obvious attempt to allay any fears in Sanaa regarding the so-called January events. Viktor Maltsev, first deputy foreign minister, was sent to the YAR at the end of January and simultaneously North Yemen's deputy foreign minister, Muhammad Sa'id at Attar, travelled to Moscow. April saw the visit of a YAR military delegation that went to study indoctrinational techniques and in May a YAR parliamentary delegation was "warmly" received in Moscow. In July, the Soviet delegation which had visited Aden then went on to meet wih YAR officials in Sanaa.

Moscow also kept up its extensive contacts with Kuwait. In February, Prime Minister Ryzhkov met with the visiting Kuwaiti oil minister to

CHART 1
SOVIET BILATERAL CONTACTS WITH GULF STATES
1984

MONTH / COUNTRY	JAN	FEB	MAR	APR	MAY	JUN	JUL	AUG	SEP	OCT	NOV	DEC
U.A.E.												
OMAN												
KUWAIT					#	#	+	+				+#
Y.A.R.			#				#	## *		#	+	
P.D.R.Y.	#	**				#	+	+* ##		## **	#	##

(+) MILITARY — MEETINGS AND TOURS OF MILITARY OFFICIALS.

(∗) ECONOMIC — TRADE DELEGATIONS, ECONOMIC OFFICIALS, AND BILATERAL ECONOMIC COOPERATION AGREEMENTS.

(#) DIPLOMATIC — AMBASSADORIAL MEETINGS, PARLIAMENTARY DELEGATIONS, HIGH LEVEL (FOREIGN MINISTERS OR PRIME MINISTERS/PRESIDENTS), AND PARTY–TO–PARTY CONTACTS.

negotiate a new economic protocol. In April, the new Kuwaiti ambassador to the USSR presented his credentials and in May he met with Vladimir Polyakov. As the Gulf War again heated up in the fall, and as Kuwait found itself increasingly the object of Shi'i terrorism, the Kuwaiti under secretary of the interior held security talks with Soviet officials in Moscow on September 22 and 23, 1986. This was perhaps a foreshadowing of the negotiations to come over protection for Kuwaiti ships.

The other Gulf states were not excluded from the political effort. Saudi Arabia received major press coverage. Moscow, which has always maintained that diplomatic relations exist between the USSR and Riyadh, took pains to celebrate the sixtieth anniversary of the establishment of those relations. *Izvestiia,* in a page two column sympathetically praised Saudi policy toward the Arab–Israeli dispute.[28] Again in September, the Soviets directed their media attention toward Riyadh. A Radio Moscow commentary in Arabic lamented the absence of "nor-

CHART 2
SOVIET BILATERAL CONTACTS WITH GULF STATES
1985

MONTH / COUNTRY	JAN	FEB	MAR	APR	MAY	JUN	JUL	AUG	SEP	OCT	NOV	DEC
U.A.E.											#	
OMAN								#				
KUWAIT	#										*#	*
Y.A.R.		#	#		*#				*			
P.D.R.Y.	**		*# #	*#	##	*	#			+	*	#

(+) MILITARY – MEETINGS AND TOURS OF MILITARY OFFICIALS.

(*) ECONOMIC – TRADE DELEGATIONS, ECONOMIC OFFICIALS, AND BILATERAL ECONOMIC COOPERATION AGREEMENTS.

(#) DIPLOMATIC – AMBASSADORIAL MEETINGS, PARLIAMENTARY DELEGATIONS, HIGH LEVEL (FOREIGN MINISTERS OR PRIME MINISTERS/PRESIDENTS), AND PARTY–TO– PARTY CONTACTS.

mal" relations, but noted that there had been contacts between the two. It stated further that the USSR was ready to develop relations.[29]

The 1986 cultivation effort was accompanied by significant events in the Arab world which affected Soviet fortunes in the region. Even prior to the turmoil in Aden, Moscow watched cautiously, if not optimistically, as King Hussein travelled to Damascus in December 1985. A warming of relations between the two, even if it occurred under Saudi sponsorship, would mitigate the consequences of Syrian -isolation and perhaps make Jordan's King Hussein think twice about US mediation efforts. Moreover, such a reconciliation might be a way for each to end its support to the opposing side in the Gulf War. The rapprochement remained on hold until May 1986, when it was announced that President Assad would meet King Hussein in Amman. The May 5 meeting between President Assad and King Hussein ended without any major shifts in positions either on the Arab–Israeli dispute or the Gulf War. In fact, no final communique was issued.

CHART 3
SOVIET BILATERAL CONTACTS WITH GULF STATES
1986

MONTH COUNTRY	JAN	FEB	MAR	APR	MAY	JUN	JUL	AUG	SEP	OCT	NOV	DEC
U.A.E.										#		##
OMAN												
KUWAIT	#+	*# *		#	*							
Y.A.R.	*# *	##	#	+	+	#	#	*	#			
P.D.R.Y.	#	*# *#	## *#	#* *		##	## *		#	##	#	##

(+) MILITARY — MEETINGS AND TOURS OF MILITARY OFFICIALS.

(∗) ECONOMIC — TRADE DELEGATIONS, ECONOMIC OFFICIALS, AND BILATERAL ECONOMIC COOPERATION AGREEMENTS.

(#) DIPLOMATIC — AMBASSADORIAL MEETINGS, PARLIAMENTARY DELEGATIONS, HIGH LEVEL (FOREIGN MINISTERS OR PRIME MINISTERS/PRESIDENTS), AND PARTY-TO-PARTY CONTACTS.

During this period, the Syrian–Iranian alliance manifested increasing strains. Damascus and Iran had agreed in 1982 that in return for Syrian closure of the Iraqi pipeline, Iran would supply one million tons of oil free, plus five million at discount per year. In the spring of 1986, Syria, having been embroiled in Lebanon since 1976, attempted to crack down on Hezbollah, the Iranian-supported terrorist group. Teheran, to show its displeasure, announced a cut in Syrian oil supplies. Syria had already accumulated a $1.5 billion debt. Damascus's mounting economic crisis was exacerbated by cuts in its Arab subsidies. Angered by Assad's support of Iran and alarmed by the successful Fao offensive, most Arab League states ceased their financial support to Syria.

For all these reasons, Assad appeared to be changing course; it seemed clear that he was intent on reducing his isolation in the Arab world. There were even rumors of an impending Syrian–Iraqi rapprochement arranged by King Hussein. Simultaneously, Soviet pressure increased on both Libya and Syria to alter their support for Iran. While the Syrian–Jordanian and the Syrian–Iraqi flirtation occurred and while

CHART 4
SOVIET BILATERAL CONTACTS WITH GULF STATES
1987

MONTH / COUNTRY	JAN	FEB	MAR	APR	MAY	JUN	JUL	AUG	SEP	OCT	NOV	DEC
U.A.E.				#								
OMAN				#			#				#	
KUWAIT			#+	#						*	#	
Y.A.R.						#		#	#			#
P.D.R.Y.	#			+	+*	+	*	+		#	#	##

(+) MILITARY — MEETINGS AND TOURS OF MILITARY OFFICIALS.

(*) ECONOMIC — TRADE DELEGATIONS, ECONOMIC OFFICIALS, AND BILATERAL ECONOMIC COOPERATION AGREEMENTS.

(#) DIPLOMATIC — AMBASSADORIAL MEETINGS, PARLIAMENTARY DELEGATIONS, HIGH LEVEL (FOREIGN MINISTERS OR PRIME MINISTERS/PRESIDENTS), AND PARTY—TO—PARTY CONTACTS.

Iran threatened to solve the Syrian debt problem by withholding oil, Moscow played host to Syrian foreign minister Abdul Khalim Khaddam and Libyan number two, Salim Jallud. (The Jallud meeting was held largely to discuss the April 1986 US bombing of Benghazi and Tripoli.) It was reported at the time that Gorbachev asked both to declare their neutrality in the Gulf War.[30] This ploy might not only shorten the war itself, but also lessen the ostracism of Qaddafi and Assad by the rest of the Arab states.

Yet, despite Soviet pressure and the fortuitous circumstances, the ˙Damascus–Teheran relationship was renewed in June. On June 7, Assad announced that Syrian–Iranian ties were "strategic"[31] and ten days later Teheran resumed shipments of discounted oil to Syria. Moreover, the announced meeting of the Syrian and Iraqi foreign ministers never took place. (In fact, Saddam Hussein and Assad did not meet until April 1987.) The Khomeini regime, in effect, bought off Damascus's return to the more mainstream Arab fold. Indeed, ties were formalized in a renewed oil agreement in July.

Given the situation in the Arab–Israeli arena and in the realm of intra-Arab politics, Soviet efforts to contain the Gulf War remained on hold. On the plus side of the ledger, the Kremlin recouped its potential losses in the aftermath of the South Yemeni fiasco. In addition, their ties to the YAR appeared to be relatively unaffected. Relations with Kuwait remained strong and those with the UAE and Oman were proper. The door to a possible Saudi connection—albeit below the level of a formal opening of diplomtic relations—remained ajar. Nonetheless, the effort to curtail Syrian support to Teheran and thereby slow down the war failed. What was left to Moscow was only to work on the level of bilateral relations with the two combatants: The USSR intensified its economic ties to Teheran, while supporting Baghdad diplomatically and politically.

Kuwaiti Tankers

In 1987, the situation in the Gulf was to become far more complex and to require new approaches from the Kremlin. As noted in Chapter 3, the new year began with much the same pattern as previous winters. In January, the Soviets issued their strongest statement to date in support of Iraq and in February, Iranian Prime Minister Velayati travelled to Moscow. At the same time, Moscow continued its low-level but increasing contacts with Saudi Arabia. The Saudi oil minister went to Moscow in January where he met with Prime Minister Ryzhkov. The talks concerned OPEC and oil prices, but Ryzhkov reportedly reiterated the USSR's desire for normal relations with Riyadh. Ironically, only a week later the Soviet ambassador to the UAE ruled out an exchange of ambassadors because the Saudis "weren't ready."[32] With regard to oil issues, the Saudi minister Hisham Nizar announced that the USSR had agreed to cut oil production by 7 percent.[33]

The Soviets also began to evidence more positive support for the Gulf Cooperation Council. This might be seen as a move designed to please Saudi Arabia, but it could just as well have been aimed at furthering Soviet ties with the UAE, Oman, and Kuwait. In advance of the meetings of the GCC's interior ministers on February 15 and of the foreign ministers on the seventeenth, Vladimir Polyakov, the head of the Middle East and North Africa department of the foreign ministry, stated the Kremlin's support for the independence of the peninsula states. He further claimed that the USSR and GCC held "identical" views on a range of issues including the Middle East and Persian Gulf.[34]

Moscow, of course, did not ignore its treaty partners, the PDRY and the YAR. As the Kremlin was courting the GCC states, South Yemeni prime minister al Bayd travelled to the Soviet Union for what were described as "comradely, frank" talks. The joint communique issued at the end of the meetings stressed the PDRY's support for the Soviet-proposed demilitarization of the Indian Ocean. It also criticized the US build-up in the Gulf.[35] Within a week, a lower level meeting was held with representatives of the YAR.

By the spring, all other Soviet concerns paled in comparison to the storm surrounding Kuwaiti requests to both superpowers to protect its shipping from Iranian attack. A staunch supporter of Iraq, Kuwait found itself increasingly the target for Shi'i terrorism at home and for Iranian attacks on its tankers in the Gulf. On November 1, 1986, Kuwait informed the other GCC states that it would seek "international protection" for its ships, and on December 1, the Kuwait Tanker Company formally approached the US Coast Guard to request information on reregistering its ships.[36] Almost simultaneously, the Kuwaitis initiated similar contacts with the USSR. The question for the Kuwaitis was not only reflagging the tankers with the hope thereby of avoiding Iranian attack, but also whether or not the US in particular would provide escort to the tankers. As Kuwaiti officials ascertained the extent of US protection, US officials learned of the Soviet offer to lease three tankers. Knowledge of the Soviet offer apparently sped the proposal through the US bureaucracy and by March 7, Washington proposed to protect eleven tankers. On March 8, a Kuwaiti military delegation journeyed to Moscow. Then, Secretary of Defense Caspar Weinberger said that Washington was "fully prepared to do what's necessary to keep the shipping going."[37] Three days later the Kuwaitis accepted the US offer. During this same period, it was announced that the Kuwait Foreign Trading, Contracting, and Investment Company had loaned $150 million to Vneshtorgbank (the Soviet Foreign Trade Bank). Although the timing of the loan could be coincidental, it seems equally plausible that the money was a down payment for the tanker lease.

As the negotiations with Kuwait proceeded, the Kremlin stepped up its diplomatic efforts in the region. In the middle of April, Vladimir Petrovskii, deputy foreign minister, was dispatched to the Gulf. He visited Kuwait, the UAE, Oman, and Iraq. All of the sessions were described as friendly. The attention devoted to the trip made it clear that Moscow attached great importance to it: Petrovskii's job was to garner regional backing for Soviet demilitarization proposals, international action on the war, and consequently, condemnation of the increasing US naval presence. The journey also may well have been designed to lay the groundwork for Soviet mediation efforts undertaken later that spring. At the same time, the Soviets clearly approved of the Kuwaiti request and responded quickly. At the time of his tour of Gulf states in mid-April, Vladimir Petrovskii called Kuwait the voice of moderation and reason.[38] And while in the UAE, the roving representative said that "the hiring of Soviet oil tankers or the flying of the Soviet flag on such vessels is a purely commercial process conducted in accordance with the laws governing international shipping."[39]

Then, in early May, the Soviet ship Ivan Koroteyev was attacked by the Iranians. Early TASS dispatches tersely confirmed that the freighter had been hit. Moreover, spokesmen called the raid "piratical." In announcing the attack, Soviet officials reiterated that the USSR would reply to any assaults. The Iranian attack came amidst a Soviet propaganda barage which alleged that Iran distorted Soviet foreign policy toward the Gulf. Two weeks later, the Soviet tanker Marshal Chuykov hit a mine. Again the Soviets maintained the right to retaliate. On June 3, deputy foreign minister Petrovskii said: "The Persian Gulf is situated in direct proximity to Soviet southern borders, and we are far from being indifferent to how the situation is taking shape there." He continued that the USSR "reserved a right to act according to international laws if provocative actions with regard to Soviet ships were repeated."[40]

On May 17, the USS Stark was struck by exocet missiles fired by an Iraqi fighter. Although the Baghdad government apologized for the attack, the incident epitomized the increasing danger and tension in the region. In the aftermath of the assault, US ships were placed on a higher state of alert. Soviet statements in effect blamed the US for the incident. It was a case of "you didn't belong there and now look what's happened." Continuing themes begun earlier, official Soviet pronouncements accused President Reagan of using the Stark as a pretext for even greater military involvement. TASS claimed that US patrolling, therefore, acquired an even "more menacing nature."[41]

As it became clear that both Moscow and Washington intended to assist Kuwait, the Iranian leadership stepped up its propaganda attacks. For example, President Khamene'i warned Kuwait against "seeking refuge behind the skirts of the US and USSR." He simultaneously urged the Soviet Union not to make a "grave error."[42] Iran offered seemingly far-fetched explanations both for the strike at the Stark and the incidents involving Soviet ships. At one point, Velayati claimed that the Iraqi attack was premeditated so as to encourage the superpower presence in the region. Simultaneously, a Teheran Radio broadcast alleged that Iraq laid the mine which damaged the Marshal Chuykov also in order to garner more support for Baghdad.[43]

If the dangers inherent in the Gulf situation were not visible earlier, then the events of May and the continuing and seemingly inexorable escalation made the precariousness of the situation even more apparent.

The Soviet approach was multifaceted. The tanker lease to Kuwait was effected without incident and without the same kind of publicity that attended the American reflagging effort. As noted above, the arrangement was described as commercial, although of course it was not without a large political component. The request from Kuwait—a long-term friend—could not have been denied. Moreover, the approach to Moscow provided the USSR what it had long sought: an invitation for its presence in the Gulf.

By the same token, the Kuwaiti appeal to the US also provided further legitimacy for American naval activity. Moscow could not condemn the reflagging operation *per se* without calling into question its own assistance to the Kuwaitis. As Moscow Domestic Service claimed: "Incidentally, the actual intention of the United States to raise the US flag, at Kuwait's own request, over its tankers is hardly objectionable."[44] Thus the second part of the Soviet response was to issue increasingly strident denunciations of US foreign policy in general. Even before the attack on the Stark, Moscow's Radio Peace and Progress claimed in a Farsi broadcast: "The United States will resort to any means to exacerbate the war between Iran and Iraq. Under the guise of defending the freedom of navigation, it deploys its navy in the Persian Gulf and prepares to establish its supremacy in the region."[45] The contrasts between Moscow's portrayal of what it was doing and the picture of provocational US naval maneuvers could not have been more vivid.

In a corollary move, as the date of the first US convoy approached, Moscow renewed calls for the withdrawal of all foreign forces. On July 3, the Soviets issued a formal withdrawal proposal. *Pravda* wrote:

> Proceeding from the necessity to undertake decisive measures to improve the situation in the region, the Soviet government suggests that all warships of states not situated in the region be shortly withdrawn from the waters of the Gulf and that Iran and Iraq, in their turn, should keep from actions that would threaten international navigation.[46]

The Iranians were at best ambivalent about the Soviet overtures. Although the Teheran government praised the thrust of the proposal, it also made its suspicions regarding Soviet motivations clear. The Teheran Domestic Service commented that the Soviet Union "has by implication excluded its own military presence from this statement."[47] After the first reflagged convoy sailed, Rafsanjani stated in a speech: "The Americans conspired with the Kuwaitis, reached agreement on reflagging ships, and told the Kuwaitis to invite the Russians to lease their ships. The Russians, who have always dreamed of establishing a foothold in the Persian Gulf, would be only too eager to come in as soon as possible. . . ."[48]

Finally, the Soviet Union joined with other members of the United Nations Security Council to vote for a cease-fire resolution. The history of resolution 598 is worth noting. The US proved to be the major force behind the resolution, despite or perhaps because of the earlier revelations about arms sales to Iran. By the same token, the USSR had earlier indicated a willingness to use the forum of the international community to settle the conflict. The *Izvestiia* article celebrating the Iraqi friendship treaty stressed and praised Baghdad's willingness to abide by UN decisions. Moreover, Petrovskii's discussions with Gulf leaders may also have included the subject of a UN resolution. As noted above, the Stark incident and the attack on the Soviet freighter confirmed the explosive nature of the war and of superpower involvement. Therefore, in addition to issuing demilitarization proposals, Soviet officials spoke increasingly of the need for UN action. On July 4, Soviet foreign ministry spokesman, Gennady Gerasimov, advocated "uniting the efforts of the international community."[49] A few days prior, in an interview with the Kuwaiti *Al Ra'y Al 'Amm*, Aleksandr Ivanov (identified as chief of the "Arab Gulf Section" in the foreign ministry) not only urged UN action, but also spoke of UN forces being deployed in the region. "The Security Council has the power to force the two sides to cease fire and has the means to protect security and navigation in the Gulf, even if circumstances dictate that UN forces be formed for this purpose."[50]

The resolution was decided on June 21 and passed unanimously by the Security Council on July 20. Although it stopped short of imposing sanctions, the UNSC resolution 598 was the strongest to date. It stated in part:

The Security Council: 1. demands that, as a first step toward a negotiated settlement, Iran and Iraq observe an immediate cease-fire, discontinue all military actions on land, at sea and in the air, and withdraw all forces to the internationally recognized boundaries without delay:

2. Requests the Secretary General to dispatch a team of United Nations observers to verify, confirm, and supervise the cease-fire. . . .

5. Calls upon all other states to exercise the utmost restraint and to refrain from any act which may lead to further escalation and widening of the conflict. . . .

10. Decides to meet again as necessary to consider further steps to insure compliance with this resolution.[51]

The Security Council decision marked a significant shift in prevailing Soviet attitudes toward the UN. The Kremlin had previously disparaged

UN efforts and the international community in general. Now, the Soviets were touting the UN and seemed to lend their support to Secretary General Perez de Cuellar's fall trip to the war zone. Moreover, CPSU General Secretary Mikhail Gorbachev, in a major article appearing in both *Pravda* and *Izvestiia,* called for enhancing the powers of the United Nations and particularly the International Court of Justice.[52] Whether or not the Soviet proposals are genuine is open to question. The passage of the cease-fire call did provide Moscow with an additional point from which to criticize US escorts in the Gulf. When the first reflagged Kuwaiti tankers under US escort sailed two days after the Security Council vote, the USSR claimed that the military aspects of the operation contravened the resolution. Developing a propaganda theme begun earlier, the Soviets alleged that Washington was using the tanker war for its own advantage and that its naval presence undermined specifically article five of UNSC 598.

The Gulf states themselves apparently understood the Kuwaiti action, but, nonetheless, towed a careful line between supporting it rhetorically and physically facilitating the effort. They were still constrained by not appearing too closely tied to Israel's ally. Kuwait's game was to engage the superpowers directly in the region in the hopes that they could force an end to the increasingly costly and threatening war. Yet, even Kuwait felt obliged to distance itself from the US effort. The prime minister explicitly ruled out granting basing rights to the US and further claimed that the US bore the risks and responsibilities even if clashes erupted between the reflagged ships and the Iranians.[53]

Despite these disclaimers, it became increasingly clear that the moderate Arab states and the Gulf states welcomed the US intervention. In fact, many of these states came to believe that a persistent US effort could "stand down" the Iranians.[54] In addition, the Gulf states tendered what has been called "political backing"[55] for action against Iran. According to reports from the Gulf, the peninsula states have cooperated with Washington by providing storage facilities, calling privileges, and medicine.[56] Thus, the Soviet propaganda barrage, support for the UNSC, and the intensive cultivation effort take on increasing urgency for Moscow.

In the long run, the Kuwaiti ploy to involve both superpowers in the Gulf may prove detrimental to Soviet interests. The invitation is increasingly seen as a setback to Soviet diplomatic ambitions. Indeed, all of the maneuvers noted above are designed to forestall the reality of that nagging Soviet fear: the acceptability and perhaps legitimacy of the US presence in the region. This is not to say that since 1984, the diplomatic offensive has been a failure. While Chernenko was still alive, the USSR did sign the friendship treaty with YAR, and under Mikhail

Gorbachev, Moscow achieved significant successes with the establishment of ties with Oman and the UAE. However, between late 1985 and 1988, the momentum of the diplomatic offensive died. Until the spring of 1988, when Soviet officials again travelled to the Gulf—this time to explain Afghanistan—there were few other contacts. Finally, in 1988 as well, Qatar joined those GCC states with formal links to Moscow.

Notes

1. Daniel Dishon and Bruce Maddy-Weitzman, "Intra-Regional and Muslim Affairs," *Middle East Contemporary Survey,* Volume Seven (1982–1983), p. 201.
2. *Middle East Journal,* Vol. 37, No. 1 (Winter 1983), Chronology.
3. Daniel Dishon and Bruce Maddy-Weitzman, "Inter-Arab Relations," *Middle East Contemporary Survey,* Volume Six (1981–1982), pp. 245–246.
4. See for example: Robert O. Freedman, *Soviet Policy Toward the Middle East Since 1970* (third edition) (New York: Praeger Publishers, 1982), or Carol R. Saivetz, "Periphery and Center: The Western Sahara Dispute and Soviet Policy Toward the Middle East" (Paper presented at the American Association for the Advancement of Slavic Studies, Kansas City, October, 1983).
5. Mark N. Katz, *Russia and Arabia* (Baltimore: Johns Hopkins University Press, 1986), p. 164.
6. "Joint Soviet-Kuwaiti Communique," *Pravda,* April 26, 1981, p. 4.
7. *Washington Post,* June 16, 1984, p. A20.
8. KUNA, July 10, 1984 in *FBIS SOV* 84 135, July 12, 1984, p. H4.
9. *Washington Post,* July 13, 1984, p. A1. It should be noted that the US options package was of a much smaller scale.
10. KUNA, July 11, 1984, *FBIS SOV* 84 135, July 12, 1984, p. H2.
11. A. Primakov, "Saudovskaia Arabiia: neft' i politika," *Mirovaia Ekonomika i Mezhdunarodnye Otnosheniia,* No. 6, 1980, pp. 130–131.
12. *Vneshnaia torgovlia SSSR, 1983* (Moscow: Finansy i statistiki, 1984).
13. Robert O. Freedman, "Soviet Policy Toward the Persian Gulf From the Outbreak of the Iran–Iraq War to the Death of Konstantin Chernenko," in William J. Olsen, ed., *US Strategic Interests in the Gulf Region* (Boulder, Colo.: Westview Press, 1987), p. 67.
14. *Pravda,* October 10, 1984, p. 2.
15. A comparison of the dinner speeches delivered by the late Konstantin Chernenko and by President As-Salih following the treaty signing reveal an undercurrent of differences. Chernenko's speech emphasized the Palestinian question and the perennial Soviet proposal for an international conference on the Middle East; ironically, it contained no mention of the Gulf War. Salih, in his speech, stressed the nonaligned nature of the region. He stated that the Red Sea area is the responsibility of the regional actors alone and rejected all military groupings and foreign bases.
16. TASS, October 9, 1984, *FBIS SOV* 84 197, October 10, 1984, p. H6.

17. TASS, September 26, 1985, *FBIS SOV* 85 187, September 26, 1985, p. H1.

18. *Pravda,* October 8, 1985, p. 4 in *FBIS SOV* 85 197, October 10, 1985, p. H3.

19. Muscat Domestic Service, September 28, 1985, *FBIS MEA* 85 189, September 30, 1985, p. C2.

20. *New York Times,* March 25, 1985, p. A1, A8.

21. "Meeting in Muscat," *Krasnaia zvezda,* November 13, 1985, p. 3.

22. Jeddah, *'UKAZ,* January 24, 1986, p. 6 in *FBIS MEA* 86 030, February 13, 1986, p. C2. Italics added.

23. David Pollack, "Moscow and Aden: Coping with a Coup," *Problems of Communism,* Vol. XXXV, May–June 1986, p. 52.

24. Al Shariqah, *Al Khalij,* January 26, 1986, pp. 1, 17, in *FBIS MEA* 87 017, January 27, 1986, pp. C7–8.

25. Al Shariqah, *Al Khalij,* January 26, 1986, pp. 1, 17, in *FBIS MEA* 86 017, January 27, 1986, pp. C7–8 and Paris Domestic Service, January 27, 1986, *FBIS MEA* 86 018, January 28, 1986, p. C8.

26. TASS, March 3, 1986, *FBIS SOV* 86 045, Supp. 049, March 7, 1986, p. O8.

27. *Pravda,* March 6, 1986, p. 8.

28. "Invariable Principles," *Izvestiia,* February 17, 1986, p. 2.

29. Radio Moscow, September 23, 1986, *FBIS SOV* 86 185, September 24, 1986, pp. H2–3.

30. See for example, KUNA, May 27, 1986 in *FBIS SOV* 86 101, p. H5; or Jonathan C. Randal, "Syrian Changes Hinted," *Washington Post,* May 29, 1986, p. A26.

31. *Washington Post,* June 8, 1986, p. A25.

32. Dubai, *Al Bayan,* January 31, 1987, pp. 1, 17 in *FBIS MEA* 87 022, February 3, 1987, p. F1.

33. Agence France Press, January 23, 1987, *FBIS SOV* 87 015, January 23, 1987, p. H2.

34. KUNA, February 12, 1987, *FBIS SOV* 87 030, February 13, 1987, p. H6.

35. *Pravda,* February 13, 1987, p. 4.

36. *New York Times,* Sunday, August 23, 1987, p. 12.

37. Associated Press Wire, March 23, 1987.

38. KUNA, April 19, 1987, *FBIS MEA* 87 075, April 20, 1987, pp. C2–3.

39. WAKH, April 21, 1987, *FBIS MEA* 87 077, April 22, 1987, p. C1–2.

40. TASS, June 3, 1987, *FBIS SOV* 87 107, June 4, 1987, pp. E1–2.

41. TASS, May 19, 1987, *FBIS SOV* 87 096, May 19, 1987, pp. A1–2.

42. *FBIS MEA* 87 080, April 27, 1987, p. ii.

43. See *FBIS MEA* 87 096, summary, May 19, 1987, p. i.

44. Moscow Domestic Service, July 6, 1987, *FBIS SOV* 87 129, July 7, 1987, pp. E2–3.

45. Moscow RPP, April 27, 1987, *FBIS SOV* 87 086, May 5, 1987, p. H3.

46. *Pravda,* July 4, 1987, p. 3.

47. Teheran Domestic Service, July 6, 1987, *FBIS MEA* 87 129, July 7, 1987, p. S2.

48. Teheran Domestic Service, July 24, 1987, in *FBIS MEA* 87 143, July 27, 1987, pp. S1–5.

49. Gerasimov press conference, *FBIS SOV* 87 108, July 5, 1987, p. C12.

50. *Al Ra'y Al 'Amm,* June 1, 1987, p. 19, in *FBIS SOV* 87 109, June 8, 1987, p. E2.

51. Text, as quoted in the *New York Times,* July 21, 1987, p. A8.

52. Mikhail S. Gorbachev, "The Realities and Guarantees of a Secure World," *Pravda,* September 17, 1987, pp. 1–2. Also *Izvestiia.*

53. Alan Cowell, "Kuwaiti Warns U.S. Bears Risk if Clash Occurs," *New York Times,* July 21, 1987, pp. A1, A10.

54. Karen Elliott House, "Arabs Look Again to Old Unreliable," *The Wall Street Journal,* October 8, 1987, p. 30.

55. Youssef M. Ibrahim, "U.S. Quietly Gets Gulf States' Aid Against Iranians," *New York Times,* October 10, 1987, pp. A1, A6.

56. *Ibid.*

5

Conclusion:
The Soviets and the Gulf

With the Soviets' string of diplomatic successes temporarily at end, in the spring of 1987, they renewed their attention to bilateral relations with the combatants. The direct arena of the war appeared to present the USSR with the one forum in which progress could be made. Except for the UN, the Kremlin might well be the one power situated to mediate an end to the war. Indeed, Moscow seems to covet the role of international broker and hero such as it played in the 1965 Indo–Pakistani war. A careful reading between the lines of the January 1987 statement in *Izvestiia* reveals that the Soviets envision for themselves a mediator's role:

> As for the Soviet Union, it has acted and will act energetically in this direction [to end the war]. This policy is an integral part of the USSR's principled course.
>   The Soviet government is prepared to give every assistance to any honest, constructive efforts. . . .[1]

In mid-June 1987, deputy foreign minister Yuli Vorontsov was sent to Teheran as Gorbachev's personal emmissary. The meetings in Iran dealt with both the war and the status of Soviet–Iranian bilateral relations. According to reports, he proposed cessation of the tanker war and negotiations, all to be followed by UN financial assistance for rebuilding. Although the early press dispatches merely announced the Vorontsov trip, Gennady Gerasimov stated in a briefing: "The Soviet Union . . . has taken a number of practical steps in a bid to bring the Iran–Iraq War to an end. First Deputy Foreign Minister Yuli Vorontsov had instructions to this effect in the course of his trips to Teheran and Baghdad."[2] According to Kuwaiti sources, Moscow was pleased with the results of the negotiations. Moreover, *Al Ra'y Al 'Amm* reported that despite Iranian objections to parts of the Soviet plan, Vorontsov was "hastily" sent on to Baghdad.[3] Vorontsov met again with Larijani in Geneva on June 30. The Soviet initiatives proceeded with discussion in Moscow between Andrei Gromyko and Iranian and Iraqi dignitaries. Iraq's first deputy prime minister Ramadan travelled to Moscow from July 1–4 and was followed by Iranian deputy foreign minister Larijani. Ramadan's talks were described as frank and constructive, while Larijani's meeting, according to *Izvestiia* resulted in "common opinions."[4]

The Kremlin achieved even greater successes on the economic front. While in Teheran, Vorontsov discussed the resumption of natural gas shipments to the USSR and its transit across the Soviet Union. In follow-up conversations, both in Teheran and Moscow, bilateral relations were the key topic. Iran's ambassador to the USSR, Nasir Hayrani Nobari, met with Nikolai Ryzhkov on July 8. According to Teheran domestic service, Ryzhkov is reported to have said that the USSR was "planning to take some important steps" toward strengthening bilateral relations.[5] Vorontsov returned to Teheran in early August where, according to all reports, economic issues were primary. Iranian press reports mentioned statements on the Gulf War, while Soviet coverage dealt only with bilateral ties. Teheran domestic service provided details of the new economic agreement. The pipeline agreement called for the transfer of 700,000 barrels of oil from Iran to the Black Sea and the arrival in Iran of Soviet technical experts before the end of the month.

The renewal of diplomatic and economic ties with Iran led many to question who benefited most from the proposed pipeline agreement. Observers also questioned who was manipulating whom? For Iran, faced with a potential embargo and Iraqi attacks on its tankers, the Soviet Union is a major outlet for its oil. One need only think back to the 1979–1980 period when the USSR permitted transit of Iranian goods over its soil. On the political level, once the Iran–Contra scandal broke, Iran was forced to distance itself from any dealings with the US. This laid the groundwork for better contacts with Moscow. Furthermore, the US naval presence in the Gulf is clearly directed against Iran. This too served to push Iran closer to the USSR. Finally, it is entirely possible that Teheran again held out the prize of better economic and political ties so as to sway Moscow to lessen its support of Baghdad. Indeed, it was rumored at the time of Vorontsov's second visit to Teheran that Iranian officials convinced the Soviet envoy not to support sanctions against Iran.

For Moscow, better ties to Iran provide the Kremlin with several intangible benefits. If indeed the USSR under Gorbachev wishes to play the mediator, then these new ties could furnish additional leverage in any negotiations. Additionally, the Kremlin may view these agreements as a way to balance its aid to Kuwait and to Iraq in Teheran's eyes. Lastly, it cannot be emphasized strongly enough that Iran remains the strategic prize in the region. An Iran with strong economic links to Moscow is less likely to reestablish close ties to Washington. As a corollary, the intense cultivation of Teheran may be interpreted as a reaction to the increasing American role in the Gulf War. As we have seen, an underlying and persistent theme in Soviet propaganda has been that the US is attempting to take unilateral advantage of the fighting. In light of traditional Soviet objectives in the Third World—one of which clearly has been to counter US influence positions around the globe—a Soviet diplomatic offensive in Teheran designed to use anti-Westernism is most understandable.

Indeed, the anwer to the question of manipulation may well be both. Each for its own reasons sought to strengthen "good neighborliness." However, the longer-term costs to Moscow could increase. Despite the desire for economic gain and political leverage, Moscow found it difficult to look aside completely as Iran refused the UNSC resolution and increased the dangers in the region. Although Iraq began the tanker war, Iranian attacks came under increasing criticism. Because Baghdad is no longer dependent on Gulf shipping to get its oil to world markets, the Iranian attacks on Kuwaiti and Saudi shipping, and on US reflagged tankers, were viewed as politically motivated. At the same time, Iraqi attacks on Iranian shipping and on other countries' tankers carrying Iranian oil are considered by many to be legitimate economic warfare.[6] Thus the question arose whether or not Teheran was attempting to use the Soviets as a protective umbrella from which to attack. More pressingly, as Iran raised the ante in the Gulf War in the fall of 1987, were the Soviets being dragged into a situation clearly beyond their control?

Unclear about Iranian motivations, Moscow sent conflicting signals. While exchanging delegations and signing new economic cooperation agreements, the Soviets neither softened nor abandoned their anti-Teheran rhetoric. Writing in *Pravda*, long-time Middle East hand Yuri Glukhov noted that ". . . Teheran has resorted to military reprisals. . . . If Iran carries out its latest threats it can only result in the widening of hostilities and the involvement of new participants in the Iran–Iraq conflict." He added that such action will play into the imperialists' hands.[7] In an even more pointed article, Igor Beliaev, the chief of *Literaturnaia gazeta*'s foreign department, an expert on the Middle East, and one who has maintained a consistently anti-Iranian line as well, wrote that Iran "is intentionally and stubbornly setting itself against the international community."[8]

Despite Moscow's attempts to downplay the apparent tilt toward Teheran, the new deals complicated the already tangled ties with Bagh-

dad and attenuated the USSR's long sought after relations not only
with the peninsula states, but also with the moderate Arabs. For
Baghdad, which welcomed the US help to its ally Kuwait, the Soviet
criticism of the escort operation was a reminder of earlier public
neutrality. This, it will be recalled, amounted to an undeclared tilt
toward Iran. In this context, the economic agreements and the reluct-
ance of the USSR to back sanctions against Iran for continuing the
war represented for Iraq a marked shift in Soviet attitudes.

These steps away from neutrality also aroused the concern of the
Gulf states. Kuwait, the longest standing Soviet ally in the region, had
reason to be alarmed because it had been most threatened by Teheran.
Kuwait expressed astonishment at Soviet action. *Al Anba* wrote: "The
USSR, which has concluded important agreements with Iran and has
appeased its regime at a time when its savageness has reached un-
bearable limits, is placing itself in the position of being almost a friend
of that aggressive state."[9] Other Kuwaiti papers further criticized the
Kremlin's policy. For example, *Al Siyasah,* wrote: "We, the people of
the Gulf and the peninsula will be frustrated and disappointed if the
Soviet Union thinks that its interests with Iran are more important
than its relations and interests with us."[10]

The increasing tension in the Gulf throughout the spring and summer
prompted the convening of an emergency session of the Arab League.
The calls for Arab League action came on the heels of significant moves
toward Arab unity which, at the ouset, pleased the Soviets. On May
1, 1987, a secret meeting took place between Iraqi President Saddam
Hussein and Syrian President Hafiz al Assad. Arranged by King Hussein of Jordan, the talks were aimed at easing tensions in the region
and perhaps at ending Syria's support for Iran. Prior to this session,
President Assad agreed, while in Moscow in April, that the war was
senseless and hopeless. Kuwaiti reports indeed indicated that the "secret" meeting was a response to Soviet pressure, while Western observers felt that the historic talks were arranged jointly by the Saudis
and Soviets. And, Aleksandr Ivanov, in response to a question about
the reconciliation effort, said: "We are also doing our best to approx-
imate viewpoints between the two countries and are working through
various channels to reconcile them. . . ."[11] With Syrian isolation limited,
the Soviet options in the Arab–Israeli disputed improved. Even Libya,
the most problematic Soviet client, moved to end its isolation. In
September, a Libyan envoy travelled to Baghdad to work toward the
reestablishment of relations. Finally, following a Soviet call for those
Arab countries friendly to Iran to persuade Teheran to accept a peaceful
end to the war,[12] Algerian and Syrian dignitaries also went to Iran.

The emergency session itself took place in Tunis on August 23, 1987. Arab leaders convened to define a unified Arab stand on the Gulf War. The dignitaries were concerned not only about the escalation in the war zone, but also about intensified Iranian threats against the Saudi monarchy in the wake of the July 31 rioting during the annual *hajj*, or pilgrimage. The riots, apparently started by Iranian pilgrims shouting political slogans, ended with several hundred deaths and many more injured. In the escalating war of words and threats, the Saudis were supported by Egyptian president Mubarak, King Hassan II of Morocco, King Hussein of Jordan, PLO chief Yasir Arafat, the Gulf states, and of course the Iraqis. Iran, backed by Qaddafi, vowed revenge.

Those attending the session discussed passage of a resolution which would condemn Iran. Syria, which had boycotted other Arab League meetings in the past, stressed that the League needed a cohesive strategy which did "not seek to turn Iran into an enemy of the Arabs."[13] The final communique did not mention the rupture in Iranian–Arab relations, but did call a second meeting for September 20 when the deadline for Iran to announce its intentions regarding SC 598 was to expire. At that time, Iran neither accepted nor rejected the resolution and the follow-up meeting continued discussions of Arab–Iranian relations. Ultimately, it was decided to hold an Arab summit in Amman on November 8, 1987. President Assad, however, declared that he would attend the session only if other Arab issues in addition to the Gulf War were on the agenda. These Arab League discussions, Syrian objections notwithstanding, revealed that the war, which had been a divisive issue in the past, suddenly had the potential to bring most of the Arab world together on a basis not necessarily acceptable to Moscow.

Between the September and November Arab League meetings, Larijani and an Arab League delegation travelled to Moscow. The scheduling of the visits was a deliberate move to be even-handed. All of the meetings were described as "friendly." However, during the discussions with Larijani both in Moscow and later at the United Nations, the Soviets appeared to have softened their position on the UNSC resolution. Moscow shifted closer to the Iranian position by calling for the cease-fire to occur concurrently with the investigation into responsibility for the war. Soviet spokesmen also criticized Iraq's renewal of the tanker war. In an interview with *Al-Hawadith*, (London) Evgenii Primakov stated that the Iraqi determination to renew the tanker war after the passage of 598 "was not the right decision."[14]

For Iraq, the signals were all too clear. In a major statement, Taha Yasin Ramadan criticized the Soviet stand on resolution 598 and added: "The presence of US naval ships in the Gulf waters is linked with ending the war. . . . Those who call for separating the security of safe navigation in the Gulf from the Iraq–Iran War harbor no good intentions toward Iraq."[15] Thus, as of October 1987 there existed a "mini-crisis" of unknown duration, in the words of one Iraqi diplomat, between Moscow and Baghdad.[16]

The Amman summit itself proved to be the culmination of the trends previously discussed. The Arab representatives focused on the Gulf War and, for the first time, not on the Arab–Israeli dispute. For a time, at least, the Arab–Israeli–Palestinian question was of a much lower priority to the Arabs than the war. Second, Syria, which did attend the meeting, acquiesced to a resolution that strongly condemned the Teheran regime for continuing the Gulf War and ignoring resolution 598. Because this came at a time when the Arab world viewed Moscow as having tilted toward Iran, the censure of Teheran was an indirect stab at the Soviet Union. Third, the Arab League agreed that, although as an organization it would not readmit Egypt, each of the members could reestablish diplomatic relations with Cairo. Following the Amman summit, most Arab states reestablished ties with Egypt without forcing Cairo to renounce its treaty with Israel. Again, this was a set-back to Syria as well as to the USSR because as long as Egypt remained outside of Arab councils, the legitimacy of the US-brokered Camp David Accords could be questioned.

Moscow, given its policy preferences, downplayed the shifting Arab agenda. TASS stated that the summit meeting had discussed the Arab–Israeli dispute and only secondarily the Gulf War.[17] The Soviet media also noted that the meeting represented a victory for King Hussein; yet, left unsaid was the fact that Hussein, a moderate, had emerged as the leader of the Arab League. The king, who had scheduled a trip to Moscow for December 1987, was quoted by Western reporters as saying that the summit had strengthened his hand to press Moscow to do more to end the war. It was generally felt that the summit was a test of Moscow's ties with the Arabs.[18] Two months later, and despite the Palestinian uprising in the West Bank and Gaza, the USSR was still smarting from the results of the Arab League meeting. Commenting on the new coalitions in the Middle East, a *Pravda* commentary stated: "In other words, the process of restoring Egypt's positions in the Arab world is accompanied by a process of consolidation of conservative forces in the region."[19] The summit and its aftermath was just one more indication of how profoundly the Gulf War was affecting Middle East politics and, therefore, Soviet policy as well.

Although the on-going Palestinian uprising has shifted Arab focus— at least partially—back to the Arab–Israeli dispute, the pressures of the now eight-year-old tightrope walk resulting from the war and its attendant difficulties linger. By the end of 1987, the USSR launched a new UN initiative designed to recoup some of Moscow's lost stature and to reduce the US naval presence in the Gulf. Implicitly linking this move with their support of the punitive parts of 598, the Soviets proposed the creation of a UN naval force to patrol Gulf waters and to prevent arms shipments to Iran. The US did not reject the move out of hand, but many inside and outside the government saw it as a stalling tactic. Some of the Gulf states half-heartedly endorsed the Soviet proposal. Yet, this tentative success must be viewed against the prolongation of the war itself.

In the winter of 1988, the situation in the region began to change. In January, Gorbachev announced that a Soviet withdrawal from Afghanistan could begin May 15, if a UN-sponsored agreement among Afghanistan, Pakistan, the US, and the USSR could be reached by March 15. Although the original deadline was not met, the Soviets continued to seek a way out. Finally, after an April mini-summit between Afghan party secretary Najibullah and Gorbachev in Tashkent, the two announced agreement on the terms of a withdrawal. The UN-sponsored agreement calling for a Soviet withdrawal and the resettlement of refugees quickly followed. With the Soviet involvement in the Afghan War winding down, Moscow has removed one of the irritants in its relations with the Arab Gulf states. Indeed, even prior to the signing of the accords, Moscow sent its emissaries to the Gulf to explain the negotiations and its objectives. The Afghan-oriented agenda of these meetings may also be seen as a pretext for expanding the much desired bilateral relations. Finally, the Soviets used the occasion of these meetings to garner support for their proposal for a UN flotilla in the Gulf.

In addition, the USSR has at the least attenuated, if not severed, the link between its prestige and the fate of the Kabul government. Moscow obviously hoped that this aspect of the settlement could ease the tensions surrounding Afghanistan in the Soviet–Iranian relationship. However, the Iranians condemned the accords because they meant less support to the mujaheedin. Moreover, they charged that the agreement illustrated the collusion between the two superpowers to achieve world domination over the Third World.[20]

Iranian criticisms of the "new thinking" about Afghanistan, Iraqi wariness about Soviet motivations, and US-Iranian clashes in the Gulf all highlighted the continuing dangers for Moscow of the Iran–Iraq War. During this same period, the so-called war of the cities between Iran and Iraq was renewed. Each side seemed more determined than ever to make the war even more costly to the other's civilian population. Soviet concern over this round of escalation was magnified when

Iranians in Teheran stormed the USSR embassy to protest Iraqi use of Soviet SCUD missiles to attack Teheran. The Iranian press agency reported that a group of worshippers, following Friday prayers, marched on the Soviet embassy chanting death to Russia.[21] Moscow claimed that the Iraqis themselves had modified the missiles to enhance their range. TASS reported a "crowd of unruly elements," while Moscow radio in Farsi talked of "provocative" actions against the Soviet Union. Moscow radio also issued a not-so-veiled threat to Teheran that these actions could undo the renewal in Soviet–Iranian economic relations.[22]

This strain in Soviet–Iranian ties was but one of the problems that the prolongation of the war presented to the Kremlin. Additionally, the continuation of the state of war raised the possibility that the US would be able to consolidate its presence in the area and possibly to recoup some of the losses sustained when the Shah fell. Indeed, it can be argued that in light of the withdrawal from Afghanistan, the superpower balance in the region appeared to have shifted even more decisively. As late as the end of April, the Soviet Union was still pushing for its proposed UN naval force. Finally, the war continued to create problems for Soviet policy in the rest of the Middle East. Not only was Moscow forced to deal with changing alignments in the Arab world, but it also seemed to be incurring Arab anger as the balancing act became more difficult.

For all these reasons, it would seem that Soviet calls for an end to the conflict were genuine. Throughout the eight years of the conflict, Moscow wanted neither an Iranian nor an Iraqi victory. The best possible resolution of the policy dilemmas facing the USSR would be a mediated settlement that would include a return to the *status quo ante*. The least acceptable end—despite the renewed economic contacts—would have been an Iranian victory. A victory by Teheran would deepen the shadow cast by Islamic fundamentalism and would present a major danger to the Gulf states. Moreover, an Iraqi defeat would cost the Soviets their standing (already damaged) as supporters of the Arab cause. By the same token, the USSR would not be pleased either by an Iraqi victory. Baghdad has, since the mid-seventies, demonstrated its independence and desire to be a major force both in the Gulf and in the Middle East as a whole. A victory for Saddam Hussein would enhance this independence and render Baghdad an even less pliable Soviet client than it is today. When it appeared that Baghdad could win a quick, decisive victory, Moscow tilted toward Teheran. However, once the Iranians went on the offensive in 1982, the USSR resumed arms deliveries to Iraq and began condemning Iranian domestic and foreign policies. The need to support the underdog intensified in 1986 as Iran began a series of offensives designed to capture Basra. Although the Soviets have had their differences with Saddam Hussein, they could not afford to let Basra, or even worse the Hussein regime, fall to an Iranian advance. Thus, we see the greater tilt toward Baghdad during the spring, 1987. Finally, by summer of 1987 when it became apparent that the US and the West Europeans would stand their ground against Iran, the Soviets renewed their "good neighborly" ties to Teheran. These links were enhanced still further as Iraq scored major battlefield successes in the spring of 1988.

This careful balancing act designed to promote a return to the pre-war situation continues. Moscow claimed that it was unwilling to enforce an arms embargo against Iran because it feared that that would increase Teheran's obstinance. This same move signalled to Iraq that Moscow would not sever its connections with the Khomeini regime. Throughout June and into July 1988, the Kremlin apparently kept hoping that the Iranian government would recognize the costliness of the war and accede to resolution 598. In the end, it took the US downing of the Iran Air airbus to trigger a change in Teheran's position.

The incident elicited very careful Soviet criticism. Although the USSR could, of course, blame the war and the massive US presence for the disaster, there were the echoes of the Soviet downing of KAL 007. Thus, in the aftermath of the shoot-down, Vorontsov met with Iranian ambassador Nobari in Moscow at the latter's request. The Supreme Soviet sent condolences and the Soviet Muslim board did so as well. Beyond using the incident to augment the by-now usual calls for a US withdrawal, Moscow could not easily blast the United States without calling into question its own actions five years earlier.

Two weeks later, on July 18, Teheran announced its willingness to accept resolution 598. At first, TASS issued only a terse announcement of the Iranian position. The next day, Gennady Gerasimov expressed "profound satisfaction" at the turn of events.[23] In the days following the Iranian announcement, UN Secretary General Perez de Cuellar worked with Velayati and Aziz to iron out details of the cease-fire—to take effect on August 20. The Iraqis demanded direct negotiations. At first the Iranians rejected the demand and it looked as if the agreement would fall apart; but, then Saddam Hussein withdrew the demand in return for an Iranian pledge to enter into direct talks immediately following the implementation of the cease-fire.

Simultaneously with the first Iranian announcement, Yuli Vorontsov travelled to the war zone. He arrived in Baghdad on the seventeenth and spent the twentieth to the twenty-second of July in Teheran. According to several reports, Vorontsov again offered the auspices of the Soviet Union to mediate between the two combatants. Iranian officials apparently rejected the offer. In fact, Besherati, in an interview blasted the USSR and its policies and in effect laughed at the Soviet mediation offer.

> Meanwhile, the Soviet Union has recently announced that the representatives of Iran and Iraq should come to the Soviet Union and negotiate with each other. This should take place under the Soviet flag. In this way the Soviet Union wants to give the appearance that it is impartial in this war, and to take advantage of this opportunity to be in a position to use its influence on both countries. The point is that not only are they not impartial in this war, but by the blatant and hidden support for the Baghdad regime, they have encouraged Saddam to commit many of the crimes he has committed and therefore, the Russians are a partner to and share in Saddam's crimes.[24]

Yet, Vorontsov only ten days earlier had reportedly emphasized bilateral ties with the Khomeini regime. It would seem, therefore, that even the cease-fire agreement has, thus far not ended Soviet problems in dealing with the two regimes. If anything, current Soviet policy toward Teheran appears to be a continuation of the previous three years: concern over the course of Iranian domestic development, turning a blind eye to anti-Soviet rhetoric, and all the while pursuing better economic ties. At the same time, the Iraqis are bound to be suspicious of Soviet efforts to cultivate Iran.

All told, the possible conclusion to the Iran–Iraq conflict has apparently been welcomed in Moscow. In its official explanations, the USSR claims—and undoubtedly rightly—that war weariness finally brought the Iranians to their senses. It sees the cease-fire as part of a general trend in international politics away from armed confrontation toward political solutions to regional conflicts. Nonetheless, several of the persistant problems presented by the Gulf War remain.

If the goal over the past eight years has been to avoid taking sides, then the cease-fire and negotiations should prevent that eventuality. There is, however, an eight-year-plus history of snarled bilateral relations that is a function of Moscow's aid to each side and of Khomeini's Islamic revival. The Iraqis are not likely to forget the Soviet tilt toward Teheran in the first two years of the war and in the second half of 1987. And the Iranians still see the Soviets as the primary armorer of their sworn enemy. The cease-fire by itself does not resolve the issues of culpability, the Shatt-al-Arab, ideology, and Islam. The negotiations, presuming that the cease-fire does take hold, will likely drag on. During this period and after, Moscow will continue to cultivate both sides: to maintain its ties with Iraq and pursue economic agreements with Iran.

It is clearly in Moscow's interests to maintain the balance so as not to alienate further either side.

As for the superpower balance, the Soviets are most anxious that the US withdraw its fleet from the Gulf. Thus far, the US has proven reluctant and official statements indicate that the naval forces will remain there for some time to come. Because this has been a long-standing Soviet concern, Moscow continues to harp at the issue. All of the statements following the announcement of the cease-fire indicate that, in the Soviet perspective, the US has not abandoned its designs on the region. We are likely to see in the future a renewal of calls for the demilitarization of the Gulf—echoing Brezhnev's and Gorbachev's earlier proposals.

Finally, the war's impact on the Arab world will be long-standing. Even in the face of the Palestinian uprising and the Algiers Arab League meeting, the Gulf War—and perhaps now its aftermath—remains an issue. The Soviets seem a bit more leary of Arab unity and, for their part, the Arabs appear more wary of Soviet motivations. Iran, with or without the war, is still a threat to many Arab states. And, Moscow did appear to be backing Iran. The support for the uprising notwithstanding, the moderates continue to hold sway in the Arab world and this is a reality with which the Soviet Union must deal. It has reached out to Jordan and most recently to reinvigorate its long-strained ties with Egypt. Simultaneously, the cultivation of Israel continues: In July 1988, an Israeli delegation arrived in Moscow for the first time in over twenty years.

In the Soviet Union today, a significant reevaluation of past foreign policy mistakes is being undertaken. Exceptionally open articles appear regularly in the Soviet press. Soviet observers candidly acknowledge that regional conflicts impinge on the superpower relationship. In the words of one writer:

> We were wrong in assessing the global situation. . . . Though we were politically, militarily (via weapons supplies and advisors), and diplomatically involved in regional conflicts, we disregarded their influence on the relaxation of tension between the USSR and the West. . . . [Soviet] interests lay by no means in chasing petty and essentially formal gains associated with leadership coups in certain countries."[25]

This kind of assessment may apply to Angola or Ethiopia or Afghanistan. It can be interpreted to explain the superpower entanglement and Soviet goals in the Arab–Israeli dispute. It is less directly relevant to conflicts such as the Gulf War. The overthrow of the monarchy in Iran was initially seen as a plus; but, its replacement by an Islamic revolutionary government and that regime's prolongation of the Gulf War did not serve Soviet objectives.

At the same time, other Soviet statements indicate that Moscow is rethinking its policy toward all regional conflicts. As one TV commentator stated: "I think that it can be stated that just as it is impossible to win a nuclear war, it is, evidently, also impossible to win a regional war, as regional conflicts in many areas of the world have shown."[26]

If one were to sum up Soviet policy toward the Gulf since Mikhail Gorbachev's accession to power, it would be opportunism plus polish. The Soviet tilt toward Iran has been a function not only of the fortunes of war, but also of Moscow's clear desire to regain what was a beneficial political and primarily economic relationship. This was a risky policy given Soviet relations with Iraq and Moscow's ties with the rest of the Arab world. Yet, the Kremlin downplayed the risks and the oscillations in policy. Indeed, when asked about the strains in Soviet–Iraqi relations, a senior Soviet official remarked that jealousy had no place in foreign policy.[27] The USSR, simultaneously, proclaimed its willingness to work through the United Nations to end the Gulf conflict. Moscow's attention to the UN as a forum for conflict resolution and as a forum through which to refurbish a tarnished image is brand new. Taken together, these moves manifest diplomatic skills not previously seen in Soviet policy. Gorbachev has definitely brought to Soviet foreign policy a new polish. This should enable the Soviet Union to begin to repair its ties to the Arab world. It will also facilitate the balancing act that must continue until the Iran–Iraq War is ended.

Notes

1. *Izvestiia,* January 9, 1987, p. 1.

2. Moscow World Service, June 18, 1987, *FBIS SOV* 87 118, June 19, 1987, p. CC2.

3. Radio Monte Carlo, June 17, 1987 reporting on an article in *Al Ra'y Al 'Amm,* in *FBIS MEA* 87 117, June 18, 1987, p. K1.

4. Ramadan talks in *Izvestiia,* July 6, 1987, p. 3 and Larijani's in *Izvestiia,* July 19, 1987, p. 4.

5. Teheran domestic service, July 8, 1987, *FBIS MEA* 87 130, July 8, 1987, p. S1.

6. According to *Armed Forces Journal International,* as of October 12, 1987, the Iraqis had hit 214 ships, while the Iranians had attacked 139. See *Armed Forces Journal International,* November 1987, p. 76.

7. Yuri Glukhov, "The World's Hot Spots: The Persian Gulf: Banking on Force," *Pravda,* July 30, 1987, p. 5 in *FBIS SOV* 87 152, August 7, 1987, p. E2.

8. Igor Beliaev, "The World's Hot Spots," *Literaturnaia gazeta,* August 5, 1987, p. 9.

9. Kuwait, *Al Anba,* August 20, 1987, p. 1, in *FBIS MEA* 87 163, August 4, 1987, p. J3.

10. Reported by KUNA, September 26, 1987, in *FBIS MEA* 87 187, p. 22.

11. Interview in *Al Ra'y Al 'Amm, op. cit.*

12. KUNA interview with Oleg Peresypkin, September 7, 1987 in *FBIS SOV* 87 175, September 10, 1987, pp. 18–19.

13. Syria's Faruq al-Shar' speech at meeting as reported by Damascus Domestic Service, August 24, 1987, in *FBIS MEA* 87 164, August 25, 1987, p. BB3.

14. *Al-Hawadith,* in Arabic, September 25, 1987, pp. 26–27 in *FBIS SOV* 87 190, October 1, 1987, p. 30.

15. Abu Dhabi, WAM, September 12, 1987, *FBIS MEA* 87 177, September 14, 1987, pp. 12-13.

16. Elaine Sciolino, "Soviet–Iraqi Ties Hit Snag on Iran," *New York Times,* October 3, 1987, p. 3.

17. See for example, TASS, November 11, 1987, *FBIS SOV* 87 218, November 12, 1987, p. 23 or TASS, November 12, 1987, *FBIS SOV* 87 219, November 13, 1987, p. 26.

18. Patrick E. Taylor, "Hussein Sees Summit Move as Message to Moscow," *Washington Post,* November 14, 1987, from the Executive News Service.

19. Vladimir Beliakov, "Comment: Near East: New Realities," *Pravda,* January 20, 1988, p. 1.

20. Teheran Radio Commentary, April 14, 1988, in *Foreign Broadcast Information Service Near East & South Asia* (hereafter *FBIS NES*) 88 073, April 15, 1988, pp. 55–56.

21. IRNA, March 4, 1988, in *FBIS NES* 88 043, March 4, 1988, pp. 55–56.

22. TASS, March 6, 1988, in *FBIS SOV* 88 044, March 7, 1988, pp. 23–24 and Moscow radio in Persian, March 7, 1988, in *FBIS SOV* 88 045, March 8, 1988, pp. 17–18.

23. TASS, July 19, 1988, *FBIS SOV* 88 139, July 20, 1988, p. 9.

24. Teheran Domestic Service, July 27, 1988 in *FBIS NES* 88 145, July 28, 1988, p. 36. Interview with 'Ali Mohammad Besharati.

25. Vyacheslav Dashichev, "East–West: Quest for New Relations," *Literaturnaia gazeta,* May 18, 1988, p. 14, in *FBIS SOV* 88 098, May 20, 1988, pp. 7–8.

26. Moscow TV, "Repercussions Program," July 26, 1988, *FBIS SOV* 88 144, July 27, 1988, p. 7.

27. Discussions with senior Soviet official, Cambridge, Mass., September, 1987.

Appendix

TREATY OF FRIENDSHIP AND COOPERATION BETWEEN THE UNION OF SOVIET SOCIALIST REPUBLICS AND THE REPUBLIC OF IRAQ

Pravda, April 10, 1972

The Union of Soviet Socialist Republics and the Republic of Iraq,

firmly convinced that the further development of friendship and comprehensive cooperation between them corresponds to the national interests of both states and serves the cause of peace throughout the world and in the area of the Arab countries, as well as the interests of the freedom of the peoples, their security and respect for sovereignty,

believing that the strengthening of the solidarity of all the forces of peace and progress, including the consolidation of the Arab states' unity, on an anti-imperialist basis is an important means in the struggle for lasting peace and international security,

inspired by the ideals of the struggle against imperialism, colonialism, Zionism and reaction and for the freedom, independence and social progress of the peoples,

convinced that in today's world international problems must be solved through cooperation and searches for mutually acceptable solutions,

affirming their peace-loving foreign policies and allegiance to the goals and principles of the United Nations Charter,

desiring to develop and strengthen the existing relations of friendship, cooperation and mutual trust and seeking to raise these relations to a new and still higher level, have decided to conclude this treaty and have agreed on the following.

Art. 1—The High Contracting Parties declare that indestructible friendship will exist between the two countries and their peoples and that comprehensive cooperation will be developed in the political, economic, trade, scientific, technical, cultural and other fields on the basis of respect for state sovereignty and territorial integrity and noninterference in one another's internal affairs.

Art. 2—The Union of Soviet Socialist Republics and the Republic of Iraq declare that they will cooperate closely and comprehensively in ensuring conditions for the preservation and further development of the social and economic gains of their peoples and respect for the sovereignty of each people over all its natural resources.

Art. 3—The High Contracting Parties, consistently pursuing a policy of the peaceful coexistence of states with different social systems, will continue, in accordance with their peace-loving foreign policies, to advocate peace throughout the world, the relaxation of international tension and the achievement of general and complete disarmament, encompassing both nuclear and conventional types of armaments and under effective international control.

Art. 4—The High Contracting Parties, guided by the ideals of the freedom and equality of all peoples, condemn imperialism and colonialism in all their forms and manifestations. They will continue to wage a steadfast struggle against imperialism and Zionism and for the complete and unconditional elimination of colonialism, neocolonialism, racism and apartheid and to advocate the complete and earliest possible implementation of the U.N. Declaration on the Granting of Independence to Colonial Countries and Peoples.

The two sides will cooperate with one another and with other peace-loving states in support of the just struggle of the peoples for their sovereignty, freedom, independence and social progress.

Art. 5—Attaching great importance to their economic, technical and scientific cooperation, the High Contracting Parties will continue to expand and deepen this cooperation in exchanges of experience in industry, agriculture, irrigation, water resources and the exploitation of petroleum and other natural resources, in the field of communications and in other branches of the economy, and in the training of national cadres. The two sides will expand trade and navigation between the two states on the basis of the principles of equality, mutual advantage and most-favored-nation treatment.

Art. 6—The High Contracting Parties will promote the further development of ties and contacts between them in the fields of science, the arts, literature, education, public health, the press, radio, motion pictures, television, tourism, sports and other fields.

For the purpose of fuller mutual acquaintance with the life, labor and achievements of the two countries' peoples in various fields, the two sides will promote the expansion of cooperation and direct ties between the state agencies, public organizations, enterprises and cultural and scientific institutions of both states.

Art. 7—Attaching great importance to the coordination of their actions in the international arena in the interests of ensuring peace and security, and also to the development of political cooperation between the Soviet Union and Iraq, the High Contracting Parties will hold regular consultations with one another at various levels on all important international questions affecting the interests of both states, as well as on questions of the further development of bilateral relations.

Art. 8—In the event of the development of situations that threaten the peace of either side or create a threat to peace or a violation of peace, the High Contracting Parties will immediately contact one another for the purpose of coordinating their positions in the interest of removing the threat that has arisen or restoring peace.

Art. 9—In the interests of the security of both countries the High Contracting Parties will continue to develop cooperation in strengthening their defense capabilities.

Art. 10—Each of the High Contracting Parties declares that it will not enter into alliances or take part in any groupings of states or in actions or measures directed against the other High Contracting Party.

Each of the High Contracting Parties pledges not to allow the use of its territory for the commission of any act that could inflict military damage on the other side.

Art. 11—Both High Contracting Parties declare that their commitments under existing international treaties are not in contradiction with the provisions of this treaty, and they pledge not to conclude any international agreements incompatible with it.

Art. 12—This treaty is concluded for a period of 15 years and will be automatically extended for each successive five-year period, unless one of the High Contracting Parties announces its desire to terminate the treaty, informing the other High Contracting Party of its intention 12 months before the expiration of the treaty's effective period.

Art. 13—Any differences of opinion that may arise between the High Contracting Parties with respect to the interpretation of any provision of this treaty will be resolved bilaterally in a spirit of friendship, mutual respect and understanding.

Art. 14—This treaty is subject to ratification and will enter into force on the day of the exchange of instruments of ratification, which will take place in Moscow as soon as possible.

This treaty has been drawn up in two copies, one each in the Russian and Arabic languages, with both tests having equal authenticity.

Done in Baghdad on April 9, 1972, which corresponds to 25 Safar, year 1392 of the Hegira. — [signed] For the Union of Soviet Socialist Republics, A. KOSYGIN; for the Republic of Iraq, A. H. al-BAKR.

Translation © 1972 by *The Current Digest of the Soviet Press,* published weekly at Columbus, Ohio. Reprinted by permission of the Digest.

TREATY OF FRIENDSHIP AND COOPERATION
BETWEEN THE USSR AND THE PDRY

Pravda, October 26, 1979

The USSR and the People's Democratic Republic of Yemen [PDRY],

Considering that the further development and strengthening of the relations of friendship and all-round cooperation which have become established between them accord with the vital national interests of the two countries' peoples and serve the cause of consolidating peace and security throughout the world,

Motivated by the desire to promote in every way the development of peaceful relations between states and fruitful international cooperation,

Fully determined to develop the socioeconomic achievements of the peoples of the USSR and the PDRY and to come out for the unity and cooperation of all forces fighting for peace and national independence, democracy and social progress,

Inspired by the ideals of the struggle against imperialism, colonialism and racism in all their forms and manifestations,

Attaching great significance to the two countries' cooperation in the cause of the struggle for a just and lasting peace in the Near East,

Reasserting their loyalty to the aims and principles of the UN charter, including the principles of respect for sovereignty and territorial integrity and noninterference in internal affairs,

Wishing to develop and strengthen the existing relations of friendship and cooperation between the two countries,

Have agreed on the following:

Art. 1—The High Contracting Parties solemnly declare their determination to strengthen the indestructible friendship between the two countries and to steadily develop political relations and all-round cooperation on the basis of equality, respect for national sovereignty and territorial integrity and noninterference in each other's internal affairs.

Art. 2—The High Contracting Parties will cooperate closely and in every way to insure the conditions for preserving and further developing their peoples' socioeconomic gains and respect for the sovereignty of each party over all their natural resources.

Art. 3—The High Contracting Parties will make efforts to strengthen and expand mutually advantageous economic, scientific and technical cooperation between them. To this end the parties will develop and deepen cooperation in the sphere of industry, agriculture, fisheries, the utilization of natural resources and the planning of national economic development and in other spheres of the economy, and also in training national cadres. The parties will expand trade and navigation on the basis of the principles of equality, mutual advantage and most-favored-nation status.

Art. 4—The High Contracting Parties will promote the development of cooperation and exchange of experience in the sphere of science, culture, art, literature, education, health care, the press, radio, television, the cinema, tourism, sport and other spheres.

The parties will promote the development of contacts and cooperation between organs of state power and professional and other public organizations, and also the expansion of direct ties between enterprises and cultural and scientific institutions with a view to more profound familiarization with the life, labor, experience and achievements of the two countries' peoples. The parties will stimulate the development of contacts between the two countries' working people.

Art. 5—The High Contracting Parties will continue to develop cooperation in the military sphere on the basis of the relevant agreements concluded between them in the interests of strengthening their defense capability.

Art. 6—The USSR respects the PDRY's policy of nonalignment, which is an important factor in the development of international cooperation and peaceful coexistence.

The PDRY respects the USSR's peace-loving foreign policy, which is aimed at strengthening friendship and cooperation with all countries and peoples.

Art. 7—The High Contracting Parties will continue to make every effort to defend international peace and the people's security, to deepen the relaxation of international tension, to extend it to all regions of the world, to embody it in concrete forms of mutually advantageous cooperation between states, to settle international disputes by peaceful means, to transform the principle of the nonuse of force into an effective law of international life and to eliminate all manifestations of the policy of hegemonism and expansionism from the practice of international relations. The parties will actively promote the cause of universal and complete disarmament, including nuclear disarmament, under effective international control.

The High Contracting Parties will continue the active struggle against the intrigues of imperialism and for the final eradication of colonialism and racism in all their forms and manifestations.

The parties will cooperate with each other and with other peace-loving states in support of the peoples' just struggle for their freedom, independence, sovereignty and social progress.

Art. 8—The High Contracting Parties will help in every way to insure a lasting and just peace in the Near East and, to that end, to achieve an all-embracing Near East settlement.

Art. 9—The High Contracting Parties will promote the development of cooperation between Asian states, the establishment of relations of peace, good-neighborliness and mutual trust between them and the creation of an effective security system in Asia on the basis of joint efforts by all states of that continent.

Art. 10—The High Contracting Parties will consult with one another on important international questions directly affecting the two countries' interests.

In the event of situations arising which create a threat to peace, the parties will seek to make immediate contact with a view to coordinating their positions in the interests of eliminating the threat which has arisen or restoring peace.

Art. 11—Each of the High Contracting Parties solemnly declares that it will not enter into military or other alliances or take part in any groupings of states, or actions or measures directed against the other high contracting party.

Art. 12—The High Contracting Parties declare that the provisions of the present treaty do not run counter to their commitments under existing international treaties, and pledge not to conclude any international agreements incompatible with this treaty.

Art. 13—Any questions which may arise between the High Contracting Parties concerning the interpretation or application of any provision of the present treaty will be resolved bilaterally, in a spirit of friendship, mutual respect and mutual understanding.

Art. 14—The present treaty will operate for 20 years from the day of its coming into force.

If neither of the High Contracting Parties declares its wish to end the treaty's operation 6 months before the expiration of the said term, it will remain in force for the ensuing 5 years, and so forth, until such time as one of the high contracting parties gives warning in writing of its intention to end its operation 6 months before the expiration of the current 5-year period.

Art. 15—The present treaty is subject to ratification and will come into force on the day of the exchange of instruments of ratification, which will take place in Aden.

The present treaty is composed of two copies, each in Russian and Arabic, and the two texts have equal force.

Done in Moscow, 25 October 1979.

[Signed] for the USSR: L. Brezhnev, general secretary of the CPSU Central Committee and chairman of the USSR Supreme Soviet Presidium

For the PDRY: 'Abd al-Fattah Isma'il, general secretary of the Yemen Socialist Party Central Committee and chairman of the PDRY Supreme People's Council Presidium.

—FBIS translation

TREATY OF FRIENDSHIP AND COOPERATION
BETWEEN THE USSR AND YAR

Pravda, October 1, 1984

The USSR and the Yemen Arab Republic (YAR),

Proceeding from the traditional relations established between them of friendship, mutual respect, mutually advantageous cooperation, and solidarity in the struggle against the policy of hegemonism and colonialism in all their forms and for the consolidation of international peace and security,

Deeming that the treaty on friendship and trade of 1 November 1928, which corresponds to 17 Jumada al-Awwal 1347 Hegira, and the Treaty of Friendship of 21 March 1964, which corresonds to 7 Dhu al-Qi'dah 1383 Hegira, laid the foundation for friendly relations between the peoples of the USSR and the YAR,

Being convinced that the further strengthening of friendship and cooperation between the USSR and the YAR meets the interests of both states' peoples, and

Confirming their commitment to the aims and principles of the UN Charter, have agreed the following:

Art. 1—The High Contracting Parties will cooperate closely in implementing the social and economic development of their peoples and respect for the sovereignty of each of them over all their natural resources.

They will promote the development of cooperation between social and cultural organizations with a view to familiarizing each other with the life, work, and achievements of the two countries' peoples.

Art. 2—The USSR respects the YAR's policy of nonalignment, which is an important factor in the development of relations of international cooperation and relaxation of international tension.

The YAR respects the USSR's peace-loving foreign policy aimed at strengthening friendship and cooperation with all countries and peoples.

Art. 3—The High Contracting Parties will do their utmost to promote the prevention of war, primarily nuclear war, the preservation and consolidation of world peace and the security of peoples, relaxation of international tension, the peaceful settlement of disputes, and the elimination of any manifestations of a policy of diktat from the practice of international relations.

They will cooperate actively in resolving the tasks of ending the arms race, to the point of universal and complete disarmament, including nuclear disarmament, under effective international control.

Art. 4—The High Contracting Parties will continue the struggle against colonialism, neocolonialism, and racism in all its forms and manifestations, including Zionism, and will also act with a view to implementing in full the UN Declaration on granting independence to colonial countries and peoples.

The parties will cooperate in the cause of assisting the peoples' just struggle to ensure their sovereignty, freedom, and independence.

Art. 5—The High Contracting Parties will consult each other on international problems which affect both countries' interests.

Art. 6—Each of the High Contracting Parties declares that it will not take part in actions directed against the other High Contracting Party.

Art. 7—The High Contracting Parties declare that the provisions of the present treaty do not conflict with their commitments under international treaties already in force.

Art. 8—Any questions which may arise between the High Contracting Parties regarding the interpretation or application of any provision of the present treaty will be settled bilaterally in a spirit of friendship, mutual respect, and mutual understanding.

Art. 9—The present treaty is concluded for a period of 20 years.

If during the 6 months prior to the expiry of the fixed period neither of the high contracting parties declares its desire to suspend the treaty's operation, it will remain in force for successive 5-year periods unless one of the High Contracting Parties provides written notification of its intention to suspend its operation during the 6 months prior to the expiry of the 5-year period then current.

Art. 10—The present treaty is subject to ratification and will enter into force on the day of the exchange of the instruments of ratification which will be done in Sanaa.

Art. 11—The High Contracting Parties will transmit a copy of the text of the present treaty to the UN secretariat for registration.

Done at Moscow, 9 October 1984, in duplicate, in the Russian and Arabic languages, both texts being equally authentic.

For the USSR: K. Chernenko.

For the YAR: A. A. Salih.

—FBIS translation

THE USSR AND IRAN:
IN THE INTERESTS OF GOOD NEIGHBORLINESS

Pavel Demchenko, *Pravda,* March 9, 1982, p. 4.

The victory of the 1979 revolution in Iran was one of the major events of international life in the past few years. It changed that country's life and its position in the international arena in many ways. Putting a definitive end to its role as a military-political ally of the US and an imperialist policeman in the oil-rich Persian Gulf region, the young republic left the pro-American CENTO bloc and took its place in the ranks of nonaligned states. It declared that henceforth it will be on the side of the peoples who are struggling against colonialism and Zionism and for freedom and independence.

Naturally, the Soviet Union warmly welcomed the positive changes in Iran's policy, inasmuch as this broadens the sphere in which our countries' positions coincide in the international arena and creates conditions for the development of relations based on the principles of genuine good-neighborliness.

At the same time, it must be kept in mind that the Soviet Union seeks no special rights or advantages for itself in Iran and that it has no territorial claims against that country; all it wants is for our two peoples to live in peace, to be friends and to cooperate for their mutual interest. . . .

It would seem that by now, three years after the liquidation of the Shah's regime and of American dominance in Iran and the elimination of many negative factors in that country's foreign policy, the great objective possibilities that exist for the development of Soviet-Iranian relations should have been translated into reality. Let us look at how matters really stand.

In the area of trade and economic ties, the figures look rather impressive. Let us cite just one: Trade turnover between our countries last year totaled 800 million rubles (more than $1 billion). Work is continuing on many construction projects that are being put up in Iran with the participation of Soviet specialists and outfitted with Soviet equipment. Many other facilities built earlier with Soviet participation are in operation. Among them is the Isfahan Metallurgical Combine, the country's largest such facility, which has its own ore and coal supplies. Soviet specialists helped to prospect these deposits and prepare them for exploitation.

Iran is repaying the credits granted to it, and it is showing interest in the further expansion of economic and trade relations with the Soviet Union. On his recent visit to our country, Minister of Energy H. Ghafouri-Fard conducted negotiations and signed a protocol on the development of cooperation. Clearly, this endeavor is in the interests of both countries.

In short, despite some difficulties and certain unsolved problems, in this field things as a whole are proceeding quite well. The existing potential for cooperation is being realized, although rather slowly. Unfortunately, this cannot be said about other spheres of Soviet-Iranian relations, which have been damaged in the past two or three years. Let me remind you of just a few facts.

By unilateral acts, the Iranian authorities have reduced the size of the diplomatic staff of the Soviet Embassy in Teheran and closed down the consulate in Resht altogether. Soviet newspaper correspondents are no longer granted entry visas. The Iranian Society for Cultural Relations With the USSR and the Russian-language courses that it operated have also been closed. The Russian-Iranian Bank and the branches of the Soviet Insurance Society and Transport Agency have been shut down.

At the same time, one cannot help noting that the Iranian authorities have taken these actions in an atmosphere of greatly intensified anti-Soviet propaganda. For example, the slogan of "two threats"—one for the south (i.e., from the US) and the other from the north (i.e., from the Soviet Union)—has been advanced. It's not difficult to see that to equate Soviet and American policy is to deliberately distort our country's policy and to ignore the real facts of international life. . . .

In the autumn of 1978, when the Shah of Iran's throne began to totter, reports appeared in the foreign press about preparations for an American invasion of that country. It was at that time that the head of the Soviet state, L. I. Brezhnev, issued a statement on the impermissibility of interference in Iranian affairs, which cooled the hotheads in Washington.

Approximately a year later the American government, infuriated by its defeat in Iran, put an embargo on trade with that country. The American Navy blockaded Iran's Persian Gulf ports, thereby doing serious damage to the Iranian economy and impeding the supply to the population of food and many other goods the country badly needed. The Soviet Union did not simply condemn these actions. It granted Iran transit rights through its territory by water and by land. This significantly diminished the harm done by the American blockade.

Finally, one more example from the recent past. Probably everyone remembers the Soviet Union's resolute reaction to the April 1980 attempt to land an American force in Iran under the pretext of freeing the hostages. The point is that, although the hostages long since flew off to their homeland, a US naval squadron is still stationed off the Iranian coast, reminding both the Arabs and the Iranians that the threat of new invasions is by no means excluded. And Washington doesn't even try to hide the fact that it would like to restore, if not all, then at least some of its lost positions in Iran.

These are the facts, and their list could be continued. When one runs through them, it's easy enough to conclude that there is a great difference between the Soviet Union's attitude toward Iran and the Iranian revolution and the United States' attitude and that the assertions about some kind of "threat from the north" are totally unfounded. However, the assertions about this "threat" sometimes reach such a pitch that people who are misled by anti-Soviet propaganda stage hostile demonstrations outside the Soviet Embassy in Teheran and elsewhere. A delegation of Soviet Moslems that have been invited to Teheran was forced to leave a festive meeing in honor of the third anniversary of Iran's Islamic revolution because slogans hostile to our country had been proclaimed there.

A natural question arises: Whom does this benefit? It would appear that there are forces in the Iranian leadership that are against good-neighborly relations and cooperation with our country. We know that the Shiite clergy, which rules Iran, is not homogeneous from either a class or a political standpoint. Various conservative groupings, including some on the extreme right, are operating around Khomeini, the leader of the Iranian revolution. From all indications, they want to slow the development of Iranian-Soviet relations, even if this would harm their country's economy and Iran's ability to resist imperialist pressure.

The thesis most often advanced in justification of hostile attacks is that Islam and communism are incompatible. This is a high-sounding statement, but it is absolutely inapplicable in the sphere of international relations. The principles of peaceful coexistence, to which Iran subscribes, are the basis of our countries' cooperation, regardless of the differences in their social and political systems, ideologies and religious beliefs. All these things are no obstacle to good relations, if each side sincerely refrains from interference in the other's internal affairs.

References to the so-called Afghan question and the presence of a limited Soviet military contingent in Afghanistan are also unfounded. The government of the Democratic Republic of Afghanistan, first in May 1980 and later in August 1981, proposed to the governments of Iran and Pakistan that bilateral or trilateral talks—whichever they preferred—be held to adjust relations, with the possible participation of the UN Secretary-General or his representative. But neither Pakistan nor Iran has yet given a positive reply to these peace initiatives. The sooner they do so, the more realistic the prospects for the restoration of normal Iranian-Afghan relations will be. As far as the stay of the Soviet troop contingent in Afghanistan is concerned, it is there at the request of that country's legitimate government, which alone can decide if the troops are necessary or not. Of course, they will no longer be necessary if Afghanistan is guaranteed against all forms of outside interference, including interference from Iranian territory.

Thus, an analysis of Soviet-Iranian relations leads to the conclusion that today they have both positive and negative elements. Many objective opportunities for expanded cooperation, which is in the two countries' national interests, have not yet been used.

The Soviet Union continues to support the Iranian revolution and the legitimate rights of the Iranian people to decide their own fate and to manage their own natural resources. The goal of Soviet policy toward Iran is to strengthen good-neighborliness based on the principles of genuine equality and reciprocity.

Translation © 1982 by *The Current Digest of the Soviet Press,* published weekly at Columbus, Ohio. Reprinted by permission of the Digest.

US ALLEGING "SOVIET THREAT" AGAINST IRAN

Moscow in Persian to Iran, March 5, 1982

The current US administration likes to portray itself as the guardian of other nations against which hostile actions were carried out in the past or are still being carried out. The remarks made by the head of the US State Department's political division on the Foreign Relations Committee of the US Congress [as heard] can only be interpreted in this manner. Once again he drew congressmen's attention to the imaginary Soviet threat and called on Iran to negotiate with the United States to protect it from these threats.

Iran immediately replied to this proposal in a statement issued by the Iranian Foreign Ministry, which strongly opposed the proposal and stressed once again that Iran would never be willing to establish relations with the United States because it is the sole instigator of all plots and provocative acts against Iran. The statement said: We will never forget the US crimes against the Muslim Iranian nation. As a matter of fact, to what US assistance to Iran are we referring when US officials [word indistinct] are trying to overthrow the present Iranian regime at all cost? It is apparent that the Washington proposal is aimed at carrying out this hostile act against Iran.

US State Department officials are concentrating their efforts on maligning Soviet policies toward Iran, which have always been based on good-neighborly relations and thus cannot be ignored. Washington, by accusing the Soviet Union of plotting against the national integrity of Iran, is not only telling lies but is also trying to cast its sins on others. This is because the corrupt US interference in Iranian internal affairs and the continuous terrorist CIA actions in Iran aim at restoring US domination over Iran.

With regard to the Soviet Union, we must say that not only does it respect the integrity of Iran, but also Soviet policy on Iran is based on noninterference in the internal affairs of that country and completely favors ending all interference in its internal affairs so Iran's just right to its sovereignty is guaranteed. The US State Department has ignored this reality and is making allegations and carrying out a poisonous propaganda campaign instead.

—FBIS translation

TALK WITH READER

Dmitrii Volskii, *Novoe Vremia,* No. 41, October 1982.

I read in your magazine (No. 30) a commentary condemning the war between Iran and Iraq and calling for its cessation. But the Iran-Iraq War is not an isolated event. It is a reflection of the rivalry in the Gulf region between the Soviet Union and the United States, which are seeking to profit from the war at the expense of the Muslim peoples' interests. [signed] (Akhmed Nuri), London, England.

It is gratifying, esteemed (Akhmed Nuri), that we agree on the need to halt the bloodshed. One could write a whole treatise on its causes, delving into the centuries of mutual relations between Arabs and Iranians and between Sunni and Shi'ite and by analyzing the political views of the Iranian Shi'ite clergy and the orientation of the Ba'th Party which is in power in Iraq. One could mention also that the paths of Ayatollah Khomeyni and Saddam Husayn have crossed before, when the emigre ayatollah was expelled from Iraq. . . . Of course, one cannot forget the territorial dispute which brought about the war. A few years ago, sailing on a little steamer on the Shatt al-'Arab border river, I witnessed a heated discussion on this. None of the conributors to the discussion mentioned "rivalry" in the Persian Gulf between the USSR and the United States.

It is proper to talk not about "rivalry" between two powers but about the struggle between two political trends. For the Soviet Union is not seeking "profit at the expense of the Muslim peoples' interests." Its course is conditioned by a desire to strengthen peace and stability in the Persian Gulf zone so that the countries there can develop dynamically in accordance with their peoples' aspirations. This approach stems from the fundamental principles of Soviet foreign policy. It is also dictated by the USSR's specific state interests and even, if you like, by geographical factors. Take a look at the map and you will see: The battle area is within a stone's throw of the Soviet Union's southern borders. Who wants a blazing fire or even smoldering coals on his doorstep?

I can imagine you saying that the Iraq-Iran War is also a danger to Western countries, including the United States, since they get large quantities of oil from the Persian Gulf. Quite so. But, in the first place, the United States is much less dependent on these supplies than the West European countries and Japan: by 15, 67 and 70 percent, respectively. Therefore, Washington imagines that it need not be too fearful about playing with fire in the vicinity of an oil tank, trying to conduct in this area also its traditional imperial "divide and rule" policy.

Second, there is currently a glut of oil on the world market, due in particular to the general economic recession in the West. In these conditions even if Iran were to halt all oil sales, the West need not suffer very much.

But someone is badly suffering—and that is the two neighboring developing countries. Suffice it to say that each is currently producing approximately 50 million tons of oil per year, whereas before the war Iran was providing 150 million and Iraq approximately 170 million tons. Obviously, the revenue of the two states, already ruined by military expenditure, has sharply declined. But why are we talking about this when their most valuable asset is being destroyed—that is, people, above all the younger generation, who are the main victims of the conflict which L. I. Brezhnev has described as tragic because it is so senseless. The two nonaligned states have been bleeding and sapping one another for many months.

Moreover, the war between them is damaging the entire Nonaligned Movement. Its routine summit conference had to be postponed, although in conditions of aggravated international tension the movement's strong voice could have had great political significance. The Iran-Iraq war has also intensified the disunity of the Arab world, and the Israeli aggressors took advantage of this, along with other factors, to attack the Palestinians and Lebanon. Washington itself is just waiting for an excuse to send warships, including aircraft carriers, into the Persian Gulf again, allegedly to protect "shipping lanes." The U.S. press also writes that bases are needed there for the U.S. Navy and Air Force and that the bases must be provided by local governments, on whom pressure must therefore be stepped up to prevent them from pursuing an independent course.

It is scarcely accidental that in the course of this protracted war aircraft equipped with the Pentagon's AWACS system and based in Saudi Arabia have been keeping tabs on the oil-producing zone of the Gulf. Plans for the occupation of oilfields by U.S. forces emerge from time to time.

So this war, as you say, is definitely "not an isolated event." It is fraught with many kinds of negative consequences—for the Muslim countries themselves and for the cause of world peace which is being upheld by the USSR. That is why, esteemed Mr. (Nuri), those people in the Islamic world who are still incapable of telling friends from enemies really must cure themselves of their political color-blindness as soon as possible. I will be happy if my discussion with you goes some way toward helping them realize that they have fundamental interests in common with the USSR and the developing countries. Indeed, this commonness has already shown itself in political practice.

At the various stages of the war—both at the time when it was being waged on Iranian territory and now that the fighting is taking place on Iraqi soil—the USSR and the other socialist community states have consistently advocated a peaceful settlement of the conflict. The same kind of settlement has been sought by the Islamic Conference Organization, the committee of nonaligned countries and O. Palme's commission. Alas, so far their efforts at mediation have been fruitless. It seems to me that it is not just a case of strong passions. The problem is also that the side which has battlefield superiority at a particular moment begins thinking it will achieve more by military means than through negotiations. Imperialist agents are using various methods to encourage these feelings. People of good will must work together to halt this fratricidal war and normalize the situation throughout the Persian Gulf zone.

—FBIS translation

THE REALITY AND GUARANTEES
OF A SECURE WORLD

M. S. Gorbachev, CPSU Central Committee general secretary;
excerpts, *Pravda,* September 17, 1987

Unconditional observance of the UN Charter and the right of peoples sovereignly to choose the roads and forms of their development, revolutionary or evolutionary, is an imperative condition of universal security. This applies also to the right to social *status quo.* This, too, is exclusively an internal matter. Any attempts, direct or indirect, to influence the development of "not one of our own" countries, to interfere in this development should be ruled out. Just as impermissible are attempts to destabilize existing governments from outside.

At the same time the world community cannot stay away from interstate conflicts. Here it could be possible to begin by fulfilling the proposal made by the UN secretary general to set up under the UN Organization a multilateral center for lessening the danger of war. Evidently, it would be feasible to consider the expediency of setting up a direct communication line between the UN headquarters and the capitals of the countries that are permanent members of the Security Council and the location of the chairman of the Nonaligned Movement.

It appears to us that with the aim of strengthening trust and mutual understanding it could be possible to set up under the aegis of the UN Organization a mechanism for extensive international verification of compliance with agreements to lessen international tension, limit armaments, and for monitoring the military situation in conflict areas. The mechanism would function using various forms and methods of monitoring to collect information and promptly submit it to the United Nations. This would make it possible to have an objective picture of the events taking place, to timely detect preparations for hostilities, impede a sneak attack, take measures to avert an armed conflict, prevent it from expanding and becoming worse.

We are arriving at the conclusion that wider use should be made of the institution of UN military observers and UN peace-keeping forces in disengaging the troops of warring sides, observing ceasefire, and armistice agreements.

Of course at all stages of a conflict extensive use should be made of all means of a peaceful settlement of disputes and differences between states and one should offer one's good offices, one's mediation with the aim of achieving an armistice. The ideas and initiatives concerning nongovernmental commissions and groups which would analyze the causes, circumstances, and methods of resolving various concrete conflict situations appear to be fruitful.

The Security Council permanent members could become guarantors of regional security. They could, on their part, assume the obligation not to use force or the threat of force, to renounce demonstrative military presence. This is so because such a practice is one of the factors of fanning up regional conflicts.

A drastic intensification and expansion of the cooperation of states in uprooting international terrorism is extremely important. It would be expedient to concentrate this cooperation within the framework of the United Nations Organization. In our opinion, it would be useful to create under its aegis a tribunal and investigate acts of international terrorism.

More coordination in the struggle against apartheid as a destabilizing factor of international magnitude would also be justified.

As we see it, all the above-stated measures could be organically built into an all-embracing system of peace and security.

—FBIS translation

Selected Bibliography

Books

Eran, Oded. *The Mezhdunarodniki.* Ramat Gan, Israel: Turtle Dove Press, 1979.

Freedman, Robert O. *Soviet Policy Toward the Middle East Since 1970.* Third Edition. New York: Praeger Publishers, 1982.

Ismael, Tareq Y. *Iraq and Iran: Roots of Conflict.* Syracuse: Syracuse University Press, 1982.

Katz, Mark. *Russia and Arabia.* Baltimore: Johns Hopkins University Press, 1986.

Martin, Lenore G. *The Unstable Gulf, Threats from Within.* Lexington, MA: Lexington Books, 1984.

Olson, William J. *US Strategic Interests in the Gulf Region.* Boulder: Westview Press, 1987.

Quandt, William. *Saudia Arabia in the 1980s, Foreign Policy, Security and Oil.* Washington: Brookings Institution, 1981.

Rubinstein, Alvin Z. *Soviet Policy Toward Turkey, Iran, and Afghanistan.* New York: Praeger Publishers, 1982.

Safran, Nadav. *Saudi Arabia: The Quest for Stability.* Cambridge: Harvard University Press, 1985.

Saivetz, Carol R. and Woodby, Sylvia. *Soviet–Third World Relations.* Boulder: Westview Press, 1985.

Soviet Periodicals

Aziia i Afrika segodnia
International Affairs
Izvestiia
Krasnaia zvezda
Literaturnaia gazeta
Mirovaia ekonomika i mezhdunarodnye otnosheniia
Narody Azii i Afriki
New Times
Pravda
Vneshnaia torgovlia SSSR—annual

Western Periodicals

Armed Forces Journal International
Boston Globe
Le Monde
Le Monde Diplomatique
Middle East Economic Digest
New York Times
Wall Street Journal
Washington Post

Translation Services

Current Digest of the Soviet Press
Foreign Broadcast Information Service
   Soviet Reports—includes Tass dispatches, press conferences, and Moscow radio broadcasts
   Near East and South Asia Reports—includes press reports from all the countries, press conferences, and from Iran, Friday sermons
Joint Publications Research Service

Articles

Western

Bengio, Ofra. "Iraq." *Middle East Contemporary Survey.* Vol. Six (1981–1982). New York: Holmes and Meier Publishers, Inc., 1982.

Chubin, Shahram. "The Soviet Union and Iran." *Foreign Affairs.* Vol. 61, No. 4 (Spring, 1983).

Dishon, Daniel and Maddy-Weitzman, Bruce. "Inter-Arab Relations." *Middle East Contemporary Survey.* Vol. Six (1981–1982). New York: Holmes and Meier Publishers, Inc., 1982.

Plascov, Avi. "Strategic Developments in the Persian Gulf." *Middle East Contemporary Survey.* Vol. Five (1980–1981). New York: Holmes and Meier Publishers, Inc., 1982.

Pollack, David. "Moscow and Aden: Coping With a Coup." *Problems of Communism.* Vol. XXXV (May–June, 1986).

Porter, Bruce. "Soviet Arms and the Iraqi-Iranian Conflict." *Radio Liberty Research.* RL 382/80 (October 16, 1980).

Wright, Claudia. "Implications of the Iraq-Iran War." *Foreign Affairs.* Vol. 59, No. 2 (Winter 1980/81).

Soviet

Agaiev, S.L. "Levii radikalizm, revoliutsionnoi demokratizm i nauchnii sotsializm v stranakh vostoka." *Rabochii klass i sovremennoi mir.* No. 3 (1984).

Aliev. "Antimonarkhicheskaia i anti-imperialisticheskaia revoliutsiia v Irane." *Narody Azii i Afriki.* No. 3 (1979).

Beliaev, Igor. "Iranian Gambit." *Literaturnaia gazeta.* November 26, 1986.

Beliaev, Igor and Kozhevnikov, Mikhail. "Iran-Iraq Conflict: For How Long?" *Literaturnaia gazeta.* December 5, 1984.

Gudev, V. "An Unnecessary and Dangerous Conflict." *New Times.* No. 47 (1982).

Ivanov, B. I. and Tamazishvili, A. O. "Nauchnye Issledovaniia instituta vostokovedenii AN SSSR v svete reshenii XXVI s'ezda KPSS." *Narody Azii i Afriki.* No. 2 (1982).

Kliashtorina, V. B. "<Vostok-Zapad> v kontsepstie sovremennoi iranskoi kul'turi." *Narody Azii i Afriki.* No. 3 (1985).

Maksimenko, V. I. "Analiz iranskoi revoliutsii 1978–1979 gg. v sovetskoi vostokovednoi literature." *Narody Azii i Afriki.* No. 3 (1987).

Malshenko, Aleksandr. "Algeria, Religious Tradition and the Policy of Revolutionary Democracy." *Asia and Africa Today.* (English) No. 2 (1980).

Medvedko, L. "Islam and Liberation Revolutions." *New Times.* No. 43 (1979).

————. "The Persian Gulf: A Revival of Gunboat Diplomacy." *International Affairs.* No. 12 (1980).

Primakov, A. "Saudovskia Arabii: neft' i politika." *Mirovaia ekonomika i mezhdurarodnye otnosheniia.* No. 6 (1980).

Primakov, E. "Actualnye zadachi sovetskogo vostokovedeniia." *Narody Azii i Afariki.* No. 5 (1983).

————. "Islam i protsessy obshchestvennogo razvitiia stran zarubezhnogo vostoka." *Voprosy Filosofii.* No. 8 (1980).

————. "USA: Policy of Destabilization in the Middle East." *International Affairs.* March (1984).

Polonskaia, Liudmila. "Major Trends in the Ideological Struggle." *Asia and Africa Today.* (English) No. 3 (1982).

Polonskaia, L. and Ionova, A. "Konseptsii 'islamskoi ekonomiki': sotsialnaia sushchnost' i politicheskaia napravlennost'." *Mirovaia ekonomika i mezhudarodnye otnosheniia.* No. 3 (1981).

Smilianskaia, I. M. "Islam i problemy obshchestvennogo razvitiia arabskikh stran." *Narody Azii i Afriki.* No. 1 (1984).

Ul'ianovskii, R. A. "Iranskaia revoliutsiia i ee osobennosti." *Kommunist.* No. 10 (1982).

Zhmiuda, Irina. "Pakistan-Islamic Principles in the Country's Economy." *Asia and Africa Today.* (English) No. 5 (1981).

"Tradition and Contemporaneity in the Social Development of Eastern Countries." *Asia and Africa Today.* (English) No. 6 (1983).

"Vsesouznaia nauchnaia konferentsii zakonomernosti i spetsifika razvitiia revoliutsionnogo protsesse v osvobodivshikhsia strankah Afriki i Azii." *Narody Azii i Afriki.* No. 1 (1983).

Index